BERKSHIRE STUDIES
IN EUROPEAN HISTORY

BERKSHIRE STUDIES IN EUROPEAN HISTORY

Under the editorship of

RICHARD A. NEWHALL, LAURENCE B. PACKARD, and SIDNEY R. PACKARD

THE CRUSADES
RICHARD A. NEWHALL, *Williams College*
THE COMMERCIAL REVOLUTION
LAURENCE B. PACKARD, *Amherst College*
THE INDUSTRIAL REVOLUTION
FREDERICK C. DIETZ, *University of Illinois*
THE ENLIGHTENED DESPOTS
GEOFFREY BRUUN, *New York University*
THE AGE OF LOUIS XIV
LAURENCE B. PACKARD, *Amherst College*
THE SECOND HUNDRED YEARS WAR, 1689-1815
ARTHUR H. BUFFINTON, *Williams College*
IMPERIALISM AND NATIONALISM IN THE FAR EAST
DAVID E. OWEN, *Yale University*
THE BRITISH EMPIRE-COMMONWEALTH
REGINALD G. TROTTER, *Queen's University*
THE CHURCH IN THE ROMAN EMPIRE
ERWIN R. GOODENOUGH, *Yale University*
IMPERIAL RUSSIA, 1801-1917
M. KARPOVICH, *Harvard University*
THE FRENCH REVOLUTION, 1789-1799
LEO GERSHOY, *Long Island University*
THE AGE OF METTERNICH, 1814-1848
ARTHUR MAY, *University of Rochester*
TRIPLE ALLIANCE AND TRIPLE ENTENTE
BERNADOTTE E. SCHMITT, *University of Chicago*
THE RISE OF BRANDENBURG-PRUSSIA TO 1786
SIDNEY B. FAY, *Harvard University*
GERMANY SINCE 1918
FREDERICK L. SCHUMAN, *Williams College*
THE RENAISSANCE
W. K. FERGUSON, *New York University*
THE UNITED STATES AS A FACTOR IN WORLD HISTORY
T. C. SMITH, *Williams College*
INDIA
T. WALTER WALLBANK, *University of Southern California*
FRANCE SINCE VERSAILLES
ERNEST J. KNAPTON, *Wheaton College*

THE AGE OF LOUIS XIV

BY

LAURENCE BRADFORD PACKARD

ANSON D. MORSE PROFESSOR OF HISTORY
AMHERST COLLEGE

NEW YORK
HENRY HOLT AND COMPANY

DC
125
P3

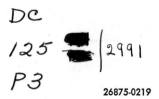

2991

26875-0219

PREFACE

The college teacher of general European history is always confronted with the task of finding adequate reading for his classes which is neither too specialized and technical nor too elementary. For many topics, including several of the greatest importance, no such material is at the moment available. Moreover, in too many instances, good reading which undeniably does exist is in the form of a chapter in a larger work and is therefore too expensive for adoption as required reading under normal conditions.

The Berkshire Studies in European History have been planned to meet this situation. The topics selected for treatment are those on which there is no easily accessible reading of appropriate length adequate for the needs of a course in general European history. The authors, all experienced teachers, are in nearly every instance actively engaged in the class room and intimately acquainted with its problems. They will avoid a merely elementary presentation of facts, giving instead an interpretive discussion suited to the more mature point of view of college students.

No pretense is made, of course, that these *Studies* are contributions to historical literature in the scholarly sense. Each author, nevertheless, is sufficiently a specialist in the period of which he writes to be familiar with the sources and to have used the latest scholarly contributions to his subject. In order that those who desire to read further on any topic may have some guidance short bibliographies of works in western European languages are given, with particular attention to books of recent date.

Each *Study* is designed as a week's reading. The division into three approximately equal chapters, many of them self-contained and each suitable for one day's assignment, should make the series as a whole easily adaptable to the present needs of college classes. The editors have attempted at every point to maintain and emphasize this fundamental flexibility.

Maps and diagrams will occasionally be furnished with the text when specially needed but a good historical atlas, such as that of Shepherd, is presupposed throughout.

R. A. N.
L. B. P.
S. R. P.

CONTENTS

CONTENTS

THE AGE OF LOUIS XIV

CHAPTER I

THE ABSOLUTE MONARCHY

MEANING OF THE AGE OF LOUIS XIV

To set off a period of the past, to confine it within dates and describe it with the name of a man or a movement is often condemned as un-historical. The stream of human activity is so continuous, so unbroken, and one event merges so imperceptibly into another, that it is impossible, some hold, either to fix definite dates for periods or to distinguish very markedly one particular series of years from any other. Objections are often raised to the use of such terms as the Middle Ages, the Age of the Reformation, the Renaissance, or the nineteenth century. No one of these is an isolated period cut off by dates, specific events, or essential differences from the set of activities which immediately preceded and followed it. On the other hand, if we are to understand the meaning of events, the importance of individuals, and the general process which we call history, we must select from the vast amount of information we possess about the past, some material and study it in detail. In a laboratory, for example, we isolate certain factors in order to determine their characteristics and qualities. So with the study of history, we find significant influences appearing now and then which affect the

3

whole course of events.   These influences are apparent,
most clearly, at a given time, and may be regarded as
conveying a definite quality or character to this time.
Thus, for more detailed analysis, we may study such
time as a distinct period or age.   It is in this way that
we discover a group of factors becoming particularly
prominent between 1600 and 1700, which exert a
marked and peculiar influence on the history of Europe.
These factors appear in practically every European
country, but they are most strikingly evident in France.
Here there is a conspicuous monarch who is an interesting embodiment of these factors, who helps to mould
some of them, and who is thoroughly identical with his
environment. We therefore, for convenience, describe
the period in terms of his name.

Louis XIV, whose reign is the longest in recorded history (from 1643 to 1715), furnishes the title to an age
in which France was perhaps the most active and influential country in the world. It is in France that a form
of government, long in the process of evolution throughout Europe, was most thoroughly developed and most
effectively applied. It is in France, moreover, that the
initiative was taken, during this period, in establishing

the form and manner of a new type of international
relations, and in devising new ideas and methods in
the maintenance of armed forces, and in their use in
warfare—all of which eventually became European in
scope and application. It is in France, finally, that
between 1600 and 1700, a vigorous intellectual activity
produced results which both constituted a permanent

addition to the cultural aspects of Western civilization and stimulated similar interests throughout the whole continent of Europe.

THE DYNASTIC STATE AND THE ABSOLUTE MONARCHY

For many centuries before the advent of Louis XIV, the peoples of Europe had been slowly struggling out of feudalism towards a more effective form of government. During the medieval period, there had been no large areas of the continent under any centralized political control, and there had been no form of government whose efforts were very successful in establishing security, justice, and general welfare. The Christian church, with its centralized, bureaucratic papacy, exercised something of a moderating influence and laid claim to universal control over many aspects of Christian life. Its chief purpose, however, was not political, but spiritual, and even in this, it was constantly in conflict with the political interests of the Holy Roman Empire. This empire was not really a government in any effective sense; its emperors were distracted by conflicts with German feudal powers, with the Italian cities, with the papacy, and by attempts to establish their authority in Sicily and southern Italy. There was no operative machinery of central control. Politically speaking, Europe in the Middle Ages was decentralized. Thousands of fiefs, comparatively small in area, constituted the political units of the time; they were governed or controlled by feudal lords who were immune from any outside, or higher, political authority, and who were constantly engaging in what was called private warfare of a more or less destructive character.

Feudalism may be said to have entered upon its decline at different times in different sections of Europe. In France, the rise of the Capetian power, toward the end of the tenth century, indicated the growth of a force destined to assist in the destruction of feudalism. Between the interests of the average feudal lord and the ambitions of the more powerful barons striving to make themselves kings, the struggle was long and bitter. It was out of this struggle, however, that modern kingship emerged. Beginning as feudal lords, better situated, perhaps, and more powerful than their neighbors, the ancestors of the early modern kings (as the story of the Capetians so well illustrates) began the process of turning themselves from a status of equality with their neighbors, into a position of kingship.

This they accomplished by adding to their original fiefs, the fiefs of vassals or those of other lords, creating thereby a royal domain, destined to be eventually known as the state or kingdom. In this process they reduced vassals, other feudal lords, and all peoples on their royal domains to entire obedience to the crown. All inhabitants of the domain or the kingdom became the subjects of the king. No longer were there vassals, sub-vassals, and varied complicated relationships between people and their highest political authorities. Examples of this turning of feudal lords into kings, of fiefs into royal domains or kingdoms, and of feudal dependents into subjects may be seen in the history of

Spain, England, Scandinavia, parts of Germany, Austria and France.

For a long time (approximately from the tenth to the fourteenth centuries), kings were little more than feudal lords "grown big," but as the size of their domains increased, and as they succeeded in transmitting peacefully these domains from father to son, avoiding conflicts over the succession, they gradually established a power which acquired stability and momentum. Subjects came to recognize this power as belonging to the king and his family. It constituted an hereditary authority rightfully transmitted, as any other property, from father to son, or to the nearest heir by blood relationship. Thus Europe witnessed the appearance of several lines of kings and their families which became known as royal dynasties. The blood relationship of these families or dynasties was jealously guarded so that the transmission of power within the family might not be interrupted, and so that the dignity of membership within the family might not be lowered through marriage with individuals of inferior rank or importance. "Princes of the Blood" and those who were of the "Blood Royal," i.e., members of the immediate family of the king, were regarded as specially privileged and of the first importance in the continuity of the royal dynasty and its power. They constituted an exalted caste, virtually accepted by the masses as superior beings.

Comprising the kingdoms or states accumulated by these dynasties we find, generally speaking, peoples and territories which have some natural coherence. In many cases, these states are coterminous with (former) provinces of the Roman Empire, and their territories are usually, though not always, adjacent, forming a compact whole; the people living upon them have some common interests. They have been, perhaps, traditionally associated in various undertakings, or they speak the same language, or observe similar manners and customs, or they reverence the memory of the same heroes and saints. Such compactness and kinship of interests we see in the kingdoms of England, France, Spain, some of the German lands and elsewhere. At the time of the creation of these states, however, there was little consciousness among the people of their common interests. A realization that they were all subject to the same master, the king and his dynasty, was the chief bond of political union among the peoples of a state. Loyalty to the king became a most important sentiment and duty.

The king had freed them from some of the worst aspects of feudal tyranny, from unrestrained abuse of power, and from the endless feudal warfare. His central government had provided them greater security, better courts and justice, better roads to travel on, and had fostered the growth of towns, where fugitive serfs might find refuge, and where trade and industry received special protection. Against the exactions of the church, also, the kings had provided some defence. The jurisdiction of the church, it must be remembered, was theoretically universal. In all matters pertaining to Christian souls, i.e., in all religious matters, or in respect of affairs relating to religion, such as the administration of oaths as in contracts, deeds, wills and so on; in property rights depending upon marriage relationship; in all interests touching the clergy and church property the jurisdiction of the church was asserted. It is easy to see how difficulty might arise in distinguishing between what was religions and non-religious, or secular. The growing state, jealous of its rights and authority, could and did clash frequently with the church. Questions of finance and criminal jurisdiction, as well as matters of appointment to important church offices within the states, were constantly arising and producing conflicts. The papacy, furthermore, claimed superiority to all worldly authority, on the principle that the spiritual is above the physical, and that, as representative of God and head of the church, the pope had the authority to create and depose earthly monarchs.

Inasmuch as these concerns were not affected by boundaries between states, and inasmuch as the authority of the papacy recognized no differences in spiritual obedience to the Holy See between the subjects of an English king or a French king, it may be clearly seen how conflict between state and church, between king and pope might arise. In opposition to the claims and power of the church, therefore, kings had to struggle to maintain their authority. Against feudal lords, also, the fight was sustained. It was no easy matter to create a kingdom. Only strong monarchs survived. There were constant reactions; a weak king, or a regency, was the signal for an uprising of feudal subjects, eager to recover their lost immunities and power, or for the church to assert its superiority to all earthly monarchs, especially against the grasping reach of the king's treasurers.

It was natural, consequently, that as soon as royal power became generally established, kings should exert every effort to justify what they had accomplished and guarantee the permanence of their work. As they had won their position and created their states pretty much by their own exertions, they asserted that the territories and peoples subject to them were theirs in the same manner as personal property was theirs. They had owned and controlled their original fiefs as personal property, and now that these had expanded into kingdoms, they regarded both lands and subjects as belonging to the royal dynasty, subject as absolutely to royal authority as a private estate and slaves are subject to an owner. In addition to this justification of the kingly position by right of possession, and the power which possession conveyed, was the traditional preeminence associated with the title of king. This had descended from ancient conceptions of kingship. From Roman political theory regarding the power of the monarch, there had survived, particularly, a legacy of ideas associated with the position and prestige of a ruler which greatly strengthened the power of a dynasty.

With their position thus based upon possession and the right of absolute control, with their titles bearing the sanction of tradition, the kings had established the foundations of what came to be called the absolute monarchy in the dynastic state. Eventually religion added its blessing to the kingship and there came the theory that kings are justified in exercising absolute power not merely because they possess the power and the prestige, but also because it is the will of God that they should do so.

THE DIVINE RIGHT OF KINGS

In the early stages of their state making, kings had been glad to receive the sanction of the church. The church needed the powerful support and protection of the civil authority, while newly established dynasties welcomed the moral and spiritual backing of the church. It was customary for officials of the church to perform the ceremonies of coronation, placing the crown upon the king's head and anointing him with holy oil, thus giving a solemn and sacred character to the person of the monarch and to the office which he held. As church and state came to struggle for preeminence, however,—when the kings became more powerful and more securely established,—the kings sought an independent sanction for their position. It irked them to feel dependent, in any sense, upon the church and so they looked above the church to a still higher authority for justification. Their subjects and supporters began to claim for them a place as divinely ordained as that of the church itself.

This idea of the Divine Right of kings was by no means new. Throughout the medieval period, when the Holy Roman Emperors and the popes contended for supremacy, there were men who claimed that God ordained monarchs to rule His people as directly and authoritatively as He had consecrated popes and priests to guide men's souls. Now, however, that there were new, fresh reasons, in the ambitions of kings, for advancing such ideas, there came a strong reinforcement to this reasoning. This derived from the great revolt against papal authority known as the Reformation. The Protestants, seeking an authority higher than that of the pope, with which to justify their revolt, found in the Bible aid and comfort along many lines. Among other things, they discovered in both Old and New Testaments scriptural justification for the divine sanction of the secular or civil power. On the basis of scriptural texts, the English clergy solemnly asserted in 1640 that "the most high and sacred order of kings is of Divine Right, being the ordinance of God Himself, founded in the prime laws of Nature, and clearly established by expressed texts both of the Old and New Testaments."

Such texts the supporters of the Divine Right of monarchs found in God's command (I Samuel viii: 10-18) to the prophet Samuel to anoint Saul as king over Israel, and in such passages as: "By Me kings reign, and princes decree justice" (Proverbs viii: 15); and "The powers that be are ordained of God, whosoever therefore resisteth the power, resisteth the ordinance of God . . ." (Romans xiii: 1, 2). Countless passages in seventeenth-century literature illustrate how widely these ideas were accepted. Most celebrated, in survival, is perhaps Shakspere's passage (*Hamlet* iv: 5): "There's such divinity doth hedge a king, That treason can but peep to what it would."

Rulers of Protestant states naturally found much satisfaction in the Divine Right theory; it enhanced their prestige in the exercise of power over their own subjects, and it eased their consciences in disavowing the authority of the pope. Even Catholic kings were not averse to such notions. Divine Right theories were accepted in practically all European states, Catholic or Protestant, during the seventeenth century. In France especially during the wars of religion of the preceding century (the sixteenth), much stress was laid upon the theory that the king held his power directly from God. Even the clergy held that the king "is the very image of God, the very Hand of Justice." Thus, the efforts of kings in creating the dynastic state and in making the kingship absolute, were crowned by the general acceptance of the idea that monarchs were kings by Divine Right.

THE IDEA OF THE BALANCE OF POWER

It was perhaps natural that as soon as royal power became generally established and as soon as kingdoms had emerged, rivalry should occur. In fact, it has been said that as soon as there were three states in existence there was bound to be some sort of rivalry, in which two of the three would combine against the third. The rivalry which we find among the new, modern states has been called dynastic rivalry. Royal families or dynasties regarded, as we have seen, the concentration of lands and peoples which they had effected as the work of their hands, their property, both land and people. After all, they were, as has been noted, aggrandized feudal lords. As feudal lords one of their chief activities had been rivalry with other lords. They had fought with them, despoiled them of lands and, in many instances, had reduced them to subjection. What more natural, therefore, than that they should continue, as kings, to contend with neighboring kings, attempting to conquer their lands and people. Family pride, motives of ambition, jealousy, greed or adventure might be the inspiration for such rivalry. Victory and conquest brought glory, prestige, and family or dynastic aggrandizement. No serious reasons against handing about lands from one king to another existed; nor was there, as yet, any grave objection to the transfer of people from one sovereign to another. People were subjects, their rulers divinely sanctioned, and it mattered little whether they were loyal to one king or to another. Dynastic rivalry thus became international rivalry, and international warfare arose as the sport of kings and their dynasties. Subjects were little concerned, beyond bearing with loyalty the burdens and losses of this warfare.

It became apparent, however, about the beginning of the sixteenth century, that unrestrained dynastic ambition might result in indefinitely prolonged wars and especially in the overwhelming success of some one dynasty. Such success would accumulate so much power that the independence and interests of all the other dynasties would suffer. The hegemony, or domination of Europe, by any single dynasty was dreaded and opposed by all the others. Thus when the Hapsburg power menaced most of Europe with the extent of its possessions, rival dynasties in France, England, and the German states worked, more or less in combination, to reduce the strength of the Hapsburg dynasty. For the safety, dignity, and general well-being of the European dynasties, it came to be recognized that there should be no dominant European state, no return to the universal dominion of an imperial power like that of Rome. It was felt to be safer and better that the power possessed by the various dynasties should be evenly distributed or at least so allocated that among the greater and lesser states there should be a sort of balance or equilibrium. This balance of power became a sort of unwritten, international law for Europe. It was particularly important for small states and lesser dynasties, as it helped, though not always successfully, in protecting them against the greed and ambition of the stronger states. It also tended to lead states to group together in coalitions, leagues or alliances against the possible effort of a king who might aim at supreme power over the whole continent.

LOUIS XIV—ABSOLUTE MONARCH, BY DIVINE RIGHT

It is in the France of Louis XIV (1643-1715) that we find the most impressive evidence of these general European conditions above noted. Not only did these developments come about early, in France, but also more thoroughly and effectively than elsewhere. France was thus a leader and example to the rest of Europe. The term Age of Louis XIV is significant.

In the person of Louis we find a highly appropriate expression of the process by which royal dynasties had come about, had made themselves absolute and adopted a divine sanction. The royal authority in France had been brought to a high degree of strength and concentration by his grandfather Henry IV (Navarre), and by the two great ministers, the cardinals Richelieu and Mazarin. By inheritance and conviction, Louis came to have clear-cut, definite conceptions of the place, rights and functions of a king. From childhood he retained memories of the dangers and disorders resulting from even temporary reactions against royal authority, when nobles defied the crown (the Frondes). He believed that law and order, the protection of the people, and the welfare of the state demanded a strong kingly authority. He assumed, with all sincerity, that he held his crown by Divine Right, and that God had entrusted him with the duty of governing.

To him, as a king, all his subjects owed homage and obedience. The lands and peoples which his ancestors had enclosed within the royal domain of France were his. The state was his dynastic property; apart from him and his dynasty, the state was nothing; it was unthinkable, even as land in the Middle Ages, was unthinkable without a lord. "L'état, c'est moi"—I am the state—was both theoretically and practically an entirely appropriate remark for Louis to have made.

To these royal ideas were added certain qualities which enabled Louis to stand before all Europe as the very type and pattern of what a king should be. In his policy, in the working of his government, in his own deportment, in the setting and form of his court, in short, in the entire use of his power, he set forth an example of kingship which has never been effaced, and which influenced most of his contemporary monarchs, and their dynastic successors, to imitate him.   Much discussion has been devoted to the question of whether or not these qualities made Louis XIV great.   In 1680, his court formally bestowed upon him the title of Louis the Great.   It has been commonly asserted, however, that although Louis was certainly not a great man, he was incontestably a great king.   Without embarking upon the delicate task of trying to define the word "great" in its various applications, we may perhaps assume that as a king, holding his kingdom at a pinnacle of power, imposing ideas and manners upon his age, and creating in himself and in his office a type and model, Louis XIV assuredly exceeded the achievements of the vast majority of kings.   Lord Acton described him as "By far the ablest man who was born, in modern times, upon the steps of a throne."   At any rate, he was an "ideal realization of the Divine Right dynast."   We may not admire his type of kingship, which has recently gone somewhat out of fashion; we may not absolve his régime from the faults which contributed to the causes of the French Revolution, but we cannot overlook the historical influence which his person and his reign actually exerted.

Endowed with no particular powers of intellect, educated as a typical nobleman of the seventeenth century, which is to say, instructed in manners and some soldiering, but with a minimum of book learning, Louis XIV developed into a man of unusual capacity. He was a keen observer, and learned quickly the ways of men; he had excellent judgment, perfect self-control, and was thus able to become perhaps the best man in Europe at the highly complex game of diplomacy. No little acumen, sagacity, and finesse were necessary to match wits with the diplomats of his day. His prudence and poise contributed significantly to his diplomatic success. His devotion to what he called "the business of being a king"; his conscientiousness and hard work in this task; and above all, his pride in doing it better than anyone else, entitle him to great credit. His courtliness and charm in conversation and social contacts were unexcelled. In person, he was well built, not tall enough to suit his dignity, so that he wore high, red heels; and by some he was accounted "good-looking." Passionate and amorous, he allowed, during his youth, his desires full swing, but in the course of this indulgence he never forgot that he was king. Morally speaking, he must be judged according to the standards of the seventeenth century and not of other times. The many mistresses by whom he had children, and whose affairs provide memoirs with much that is sensational, affected matters of state to a comparatively slight degree.

From ruinous debauchery, he was undoubtedly saved by his strong will and his pride in being king. In the matter of this pride, it must be recalled that he inherited qualities from two celebrated dynasties. If he had something of the Capetian ability and French charm from his grandfather, the great Henry IV, he also inherited, through his mother, the dignity and over-weening pride of the Hapsburgs. Charles V and Philip II were also his forbears; and the stiff, touch-me-not aloofness of the Hapsburgs tended, in Louis XIV, to predominate over the debonair good-fellow-ship derived from the popular Henry of Navarre. It was probably this conscious pride, contributing much in his earlier years to steady him, which also, in his later years, enhanced by adulation, dazzling successes, and the pomp of power, warped his judgment and ad-versely affected his attainments.

THE CULT OF MAJESTY

Translating these kingly qualities into action, thus personifying the Absolute Monarchy, of which he was so fitting an exemplification, Louis XIV created a suit-able court. A court provided the proper setting for majesty. Majesty was indispensable for a monarch by divine right. The king should be a fitting symbol of God, himself a sort of earthly image of the Deity. For this rôle, Louis was, in appearance and general bearing, not unworthy. He chose for his emblem the sun, and for his motto *"nec pluribus impar."* In the sun he selected a token representing his own position as the earthly source of light and life. His motto im-plied a status second to none. His Majesty was the "Sun King," and his subjects were to adore and rever-ence this majesty as the source of a divine order upon earth. "As the earth drew its life from the radiance of the sun, so the life of France emanated from his person."

For such a cult of majesty to be taken seriously may seem to a twentieth-century mind very extraordinary, or even silly, but in the light of what the monarchy meant to seventeenth-century Europe, popular adoration of the royal dynasty, and loyalty to it, cannot be found entirely unreasonable. The historical and natural leaders of the people, i.e., the nobles, but recently feudal lords, often cruel, exacting, and warlike, had rarely indicated that they could or would consider any interests but their own. Even they, once realizing that their independence was hopeless in the face of royal authority, came to accept the Divine Right of the monarchy, and added their support to this cult of majesty. The generally accepted attitude of the times is expressed in the speeches and writings of Bossuet, one of the most conspicuous prelates of the French church. This "learned and upright bishop" wrote a book, *Political ideas derived from the very words of Holy Scripture*. Herein, he maintains that government itself was divinely ordained to enable man to live in organized society. "Under God, monarchy is, of all forms of government, the most usual, the most ancient, and therefore the most natural; it is likewise the strongest and most efficient, therefore the best." The king's person is sacred; it is blasphemy or sacrilege to conspire against him or to assail his person. He is to govern the state as a father governs his family. His power is absolute and autocratic; for he is accountable to God alone. "Greater reason is given to a king than to anyone else, the king is an earthly image of God's majesty, and it is wrong, therefore, to look upon him as a mere man. The king is a public person and in him the whole nation is embodied." He is the state in very truth. "As in God are united all perfection and every virtue, so all the power of all the individuals in a community is united in the person of the king."

As the embodiment of majesty and earthly power, Louis was popular. The French were delighted with him, and other European peoples were impressed. He was *the* king: just what a king ought to be. It has been said that Louis XIV was the "greatest actor of majesty that ever filled a throne." We are still prone to think of a *king* as what is suggested by the name and demeanor of Louis XIV. Other monarchs did their best to emulate him, especially in outward appearances, deportment, and manners. Collectively, these manifestations may be expressed in the term etiquette. Much of the etiquette practiced at the court of Louis XIV was doubtless inherited from Hapsburg tradition. Some of its forms lingered on, at Vienna, among the Austrian branch of the Hapsburgs, until the death of the Emperor Francis Joseph in 1916.

To us it seems absurd that a monarch, who is, after all, only a man, should rise from his bed every morning with a formal ceremony (levee) in which crowds of the highest dignitaries in the land performed the duties of valets. Princes and dukes handed him his underwear, shoes, shirts, and other garments; lesser lords and ladies pushed and shoved with eagerness to attain the great honor of simply being present! It seems ridiculous that this same formality and publicity should attend him at his meals, at most of his play, during his hours of work, and finally, when he retired for the night. But it must be remembered that such formalities are inseparable from an office as exalted as that of a divine right monarch. To impress his subjects, to create atmosphere, and to give a sense of reality to the claims which monarchy advanced, all these were necessary. That such procedure was impressive is undoubtedly true. It is still so. The glamor which attends a crown, the fascination which surrounds royalty, may be seen to-day in the interest of the masses of the British people in their royal dynasty—not to mention the interest of the American people in the personal affairs of both European royalty and of their own citizens of "high degree."

Despite the influence of democratic ideas and the limitations which have been placed by constitutions upon the powers of kings, the persons and etiquette of royalty are still factors with which to conjure. The king's person is still a mighty symbol; his life and daily activities still command devoted attention. He is still surrounded by much mystery; he is still a majesty, aloof from other men; he is still surrounded by titles and some functions which are reminiscent of the days of Louis XIV. As for the passionate avidity with which people sought the honor of attendance at levees, we may easily comprehend this, by observing the twentieth-century press and its catering to the popular demands for intimate and personal details of the lives of those who attain any form of publicity by means much more ridiculous, frequently, than having been born a king.

The task of keeping up this solemn dignity, day after day, month after month, and year after year, for over half a century was no slight burden. Through defeat, as well as through success, through sorrow as well as through gaiety and pleasure, Louis never faltered. Tiresome and stupid though these ceremonies may have been, though generations came and went, Louis never relaxed or gave in; to the end, he remained calm, courteous, and dignified—the "first gentleman in Europe." This was his duty, among the lesser responsibilities, perhaps, but still it was acting as a king should act, and Louis did it faithfully and becomingly. Not only every inch a king, but every moment a king.

VERSAILLES AND ITS SIGNIFICANCE

Appropriate setting for king and court was created by Louis at the château of Versailles. Here, in what had been a barren wilderness, safely removed some nine miles from the turmoil and agitation of Paris and the common world, in a spot which would be sacred to majesty, and to nothing else, majesty was embodied in brick and mortar. In perhaps no other historical instance are the names of monarch and his palace more frequently associated or, in this association, more imbued with meaning. Louis XIV can hardly be brought to mind without a mental picture of the vast buildings and gardens of Versailles. The survival of these buildings and parks, now dedicated "A Toutes les

Gloires de la France," brings home to us, after more than two centuries, not only the tangible qualities of a real monarch by divine right, but also the identity of the monarch and the state,—all the glories of France.

Here, at Versailles, centered the most genuine affections of Louis. If the court and its setting were appropriate for the proper display of his own majesty, it was also fitting that he should allow his interests free play in the construction of the background. Versailles served two important interests: exactly the right scene for the court, and secondly, the means for gratifying the tastes and penchants of Louis himself. Like some illustrious potentates of an earlier time, particularly Augustus and Justinian, Louis XIV was keenly interested in building. Many structures familiar to the visitor in Paris still bear witness to his architectural interests, but most of all, Versailles was the center of his affections. This was his own creation, something which grew under the supervision of Mansart, with the constant attention of the king's fostering care and genuine enthusiasm.

It is not necessary to recount the statistics of Versailles to prove that the cost of creating it was enormous, or that the dimensions are in excess of those of any other castle or castle grounds in the world. To a king of Louis' grandiose conceptions such surroundings must be worthy of his grandeur. They were. The palace became not only the seat of earthly majesty, the capital of the government of a kingdom, but also the residence of ten thousand people, a city in itself. Here resided not only the king and the royal family, but also the aristocracy of France who aspired to a part in the affairs of the state. Not to be quartered in the palace was to be in exile. To be away from the king's presence was to be in banishment. Besides apartments for living, rooms for the conduct of business of the state and for grand ceremonials, there were a chapel, barracks, stables, museums and other accommodations. The planning, construction, and decoration of this great structure was an historical incident in itself. The work was done by the most competent and skilful artists and craftsmen of the day, and, as a whole, it is a monument in the development of French art and taste.

Among the architects of Versailles were François Mansart (1598-1666) who has given his name to a type of roof of which we see numerous specimens everywhere in this country, and his nephew, Jules Hardouin-Mansart (1645-1708), whom Louis greatly admired and to whom he showed genuine affection. His was the guiding hand for most of what was done at Versailles. For the interior decoration, François Le Brun (1619-1690) was chiefly responsible. Paintings, frescoes, tapestries, bronzes and sculptures were produced under his general direction.

Throughout Europe Versailles exerted great influence; it became a criterion of taste and a general architectural pattern on which many palaces and royal residences were constructed. At Sans Souci (Potsdam), in Vienna, in St. Petersburg, in several of the German states, especially in Bavaria, and even in England the architectural inspiration of Versailles is still evident. In style, this huge palace is not, from the present-day point of view, generally accepted as interesting or impressive. Its chief note is the form and proportion reminiscent of classical architecture. Its impressiveness consists principally in its size; it has a façade of over a quarter of a mile in length. A section of this front may well be admired for its proportions and its details, but when this same motive is reproduced, without a break, without any striking features, for over five hundred yards, the effect is undoubtedly monotonous. The building is uniformly of what we should call three story height, with no central or dominating element. Vastness and regularity are its leading characteristics. Opinions vary as to its interest; some think that it is restrained, imposing, and classically beautiful; others find it a "monstrous row of buildings . . . resembling its master, grandiose commonplace and dull."

Inside, the rooms in their original state were formal and imposing, richly decorated with wall and ceiling paintings recounting scenes of Louis' military, political, and cultural triumphs. Much elaborate carving, many bronze casts and marble statues, silver furniture, costly tapestries, and a great deal of gilding produced an atmosphere of extraordinary luxury and boundless wealth. What is sometimes called the architectural masterpiece of the Age of Louis XIV is the great Hall of Mirrors (Galerie des Glaces). It is two hundred feet long, and from it seventeen high arched windows open upon the extensive terraces and gardens below. The wall opposite these windows consists of seventeen arched Venetian mirrors, each thirty feet high and imported at enormous expense from Venice. Great silver tubs or vases held the scores of orange trees with which this room was adorned. Louis had a preference for the scent of orange blossoms. Also among the glories of the seventeenth century were the monumental staircases of Versailles, particularly the Escalier des Ambassadeurs. This flight of steps was mounted only by envoys of foreign monarchs who were received at the top by Louis and his court. Built of costly marbles in green, gray, white and violet, heavily gilded and set with semi-precious stones, these gorgeous steps provided a fitting approach to the glory of the Sun King.

Surrounding the château were the gardens and parks which were almost as significant a feature of Louis' grandeur as the palace itself. Most of the designing and laying out of the surroundings was done by André Lenôtre (1613-1700), who may be called the master gardener of his age. Drawing his inspiration from the Italian gardens of the Renaissance, he created for Louis XIV a park which, for a time, became the model for the world. To produce this extensive park in the midst of what had been a dry, sandy waste demanded much labor and money. Water was difficult to procure, and after a heavy toll in life and money, a supply was finally secured. One plan had been based upon the diversion of the stream of the River Eure through an aqueduct after the Roman manner. Over 1,600 arches for this aqueduct, some of them "twice as high as the towers of Notre Dame," were erected before the plan was abandoned. Water was ultimately pumped from the Seine by a colossal "machine" at Marly-la-Machine; and over ninety miles of drainage canals were dug to collect the surface water from the plateau of Versailles.

The park itself consisted of stretches of forest intersected by allées and dotted here and there with bosquets or nooks, terraces and flower beds. Statuary found appropriate settings everywhere. At many points there are basins or pools which contain the celebrated fountains. These "grandes eaux" contained, in the time of Louis XIV, 1400 jets. There remain some 600 of these jets, which, on the specially appointed days when they play, still constitute one of the "sights" of Europe. At the side of the park opposite the palace, and approached by a grand avenue leading through forest, gardens, and around basins, lies the Grand Canal. On this sheet of water, about a mile long, floated the gondolas, ship models and other vessels which played so important a part in the great fêtes and carnivals characteristic of life at Versailles. It was a favorite diversion of the king to spend the evenings, when the weather was fine, floating about in a gondola listening to music wafted over the water. Thousands of trees and shrubs were planted to make the vast park. Some of the foliage was trimmed, in the Dutch manner, into formal, conventional shapes giving an air of artificiality to the landscape. Gardens and flower beds were also arranged in formal patterns so that even Nature, in the presence of the Grand Monarch, was subjected to the regulations of symmetry and deference.

Here at Versailles, surrounded by the magnificence

of the château and the beauty of park, fountains, and gardens, reveled the leaders of France. Pomp and splendor, luxury and extravagance prevailed. Intrigue for the royal favor occupied many minds and much time, and gambling whiled away some of the hours; hunting, fêtes and festivities filled the others. The natural tendency, under these circumstances, to vice and depravity was checked by the will and example of the king. A certain decorum and public decency were rigorously exacted. Morals were not high, it is true, but such standards as there were, the king supported. No gentleman could cheat at cards and remain a moment at court. Sexual irregularities were not, in themselves, rigorously suppressed, but such offences as might become scandals were not tolerated.

It is not deniable that Louis' magnificence provoked universal admiration. Most of the kings and even the lesser princes and nobles of Europe endeavored, as far as their resources permitted, to reproduce Versailles, at least in miniature, on their own estates. "Everywhere the nobility rebuilt or extended their chateaux to the new pattern. A great industry [in] beautiful and elaborate fabrics and furnishings developed. The luxurious arts flourished everywhere; sculpture in alabaster, faïence, gilt woodwork, metal work, stamped leather, much music, magnificent painting and buildings, fine cookery, fine vintages. Amidst the mirrors and fine furniture went a strange race of 'gentlemen' in vast powdered wigs, silks, and laces, poised upon high, red heels, supported by amazing canes; and still more wonderful 'ladies,' under towers of powdered hair, and wearing vast expansions of silk and satin, sustained on wire. Through it all postured the great Louis, the sun of his world—unaware of the meagre and sulky and bitter faces that watched him from those lower darknesses to which his sunshine did not penetrate."

From Versailles emanated the dress, manners, speech, and fashions of civilized Europe. The court, comprising a significant portion of the higher nobility of France, became the leaders of these manifestations of culture, and furnished the living decorations for its brilliance. The life of this court was resplendent with gaiety, extravagance, and irresponsibility. Devoted to pleasure, flattery and intrigue, the courtiers were subjected, in their morals and character naturally enough, to a steady deterioration. Out of contact with their provincial estates, deprived of any political duties, and, by special privilege exempt from the burdens of taxation and public responsibilities alike, these nobles of France became social parasites. Instead of serving as the natural leaders of the people of France, mediating between the crown and its subjects, they wasted their resources, abilities, and time in the extravagance of trying to keep up appearances at court, of gambling with the king, and of maintaining their social prestige. Possibly the king deliberately encouraged this emasculation of his greatest subjects. By inciting them to live at Versailles he assuredly confined them to a gilded cage, and destroyed their capacity for independence, or for opposition to the crown. His own glory was thereby enhanced; by contrast, the noblest peers of

France were weak, impoverished, and insignificant. As to the result, it has been frequently pointed out that this destruction of the free spirit and self-reliance of the most intelligent and capable element in France contributed to the causes of the Revolution. When the crisis of the eighteenth century arrived, the nobles, demoralized, financially embarrassed, and without initiative were unable to serve either the king or the people, or, in fact, to save themselves.

Versailles also served to remove the king from contact with his people and with public opinion. It eventually became a symbol of extravagance and waste, of Bourbon selfishness and royal tyranny. It was not surprising that after the meeting of the Estates General in 1789, one of the early manifestations of revolutionary violence should have been the transfer of the king and court from Versailles, and its associations hateful to the people, to Paris where France at last acquired possession of her monarchy.

POLITICAL MACHINERY OF THE ABSOLUTE MONARCHY
—GOVERNMENT BY COUNCIL

In the machinery of Louis' government we may see how the Monarch by Divine Right translated his theories into action. After the death of Cardinal Mazarin, in 1661, the chief ministers of state came to the king, the young Louis XIV, to inquire of whom they should henceforth seek their instructions. It had hitherto been the practice of French kings to delegate most of the business of governing to a chief or first minister, who held his office as long as the king pleased, who instructed the other ministers, and who formulated general policies for the king's approval. To the surprise of the ministers and the court, Louis announced that he would be his own first minister and that he would actually oversee the workings of the government himself. This involved an enormous amount of routine, long conferences, dull inspection of details, endless interviews. Most kings preferred an easier life. Not so, the indefatigable Sun King. He would govern as well as reign.

The most important matters of the kingdom were discussed by the king with four or five of his chief councillors in a meeting which occurred three times a week. This group was known as the Council of State (Conseil d'Etat, also called the Conseil d'en haut-High or Supreme Council) and was the pivot of the whole government. Affairs of greatest weight were here discussed, everyone taking part, but the decision rested solely and absolutely with the king. Hence, the Absolute Monarchy. This council exercised no limitations upon the power of the king, nor was there any limitation as to what it should decide, except as the king willed. It did not rest upon any precedent, tradition or custom, and did not acquire a constitutional position as did similar councils in other countries. It was the creation of the king and depended entirely upon his will. No records of meetings were kept.

Secondly, there was a similar body, or committee, known as the Conseil des Depêches (Council of Dispatches) meeting under the presidency of the king, in which matters relating to the internal or domestic problems of France were considered. This corresponded to the British Home Office, or, slightly, to the American Department of the Interior. A third council, the Conseil des Finances, was devoted to matters of taxation and revenue. In all three of these bodies, which met in the king's apartments, he himself presided and rendered the final decisions. There were no questions of majority votes, or minority opposition. The king's will was law. Other councils existed, at which the king occasionally presided, but these dealt with matters less vitally concerning the government as a whole. The most important of these was the Conseil Privé (Privy Council or Council of Parties), which was primarily a judicial committee, vague in its scope, but in general acting as a sort of supreme judicial court. There were also councils for commerce, for colonies and for religious affairs.

Working through these councils, the authority of the king was felt in all spheres of the government, both central and local. Thus was completed the work of Richelieu, who, through his employment of the intendants, officials responsible directly to the crown, began the task of subordinating to the central government every phase of provincial and local government. Provincial governors, under Louis XIV, became mere figureheads; the intendant in each province was, subject to instructions from a council or minister, all-powerful. Provincial Estates, groups representing by classes or estates—i.e., nobles, clergy, bourgeoisie, the interests of the provinces (some of which had been in

existence since medieval times) were strictly subjected
to the crown, and were completely subordinated to the
direction of the intendant. [Provincial parlements,
courts of law, also lost much of their independence and
importance.] Even town governments, which had, since
the days when they received certain liberties in their
medieval charters, exercised a measure of local self-
control, lost to the intendant most of their autonomy.
Town offices which were hereditary, were on two occasions revoked by the king, and sold again, at high prices
to new bidders. ¯ In this manner did the Absolute Monarchy centralize the control of France, a centralization
which has persisted, and even under a Republican form
of government, is regarded by many Frenchmen as one
of the most serious defects in the political life of France
to-day. ¯

Under the driving force of the king's energy and
ambition this centralization worked reasonably well.
Much was accomplished in improving the general conditions of French life.   Public affairs were handled with
a fair degree of effectiveness.   Thus, in a sense, absolutism was justified.   It is frequently so.   Even the
twentieth century has already seen dictatorships set up
to confront situations of disorder, weakness, and
threatened anarchy, not unlike those of the Frondes
which preceded the absolutism of Louis XIV.   After
all, however, despotism can be tolerated only so long
as it justifies itself by its success.   When its efficiency
weakens, then its claim upon the loyalty of the people
vanishes, and the preliminary signs of disaffection and
revolution appear.   History, as yet, seems to have re-

vealed no means by which effective absolutism can be indefinitely prolonged. Hereditary monarchy has been tried again and again, but has failed. The efficiency of an absolute monarch does not necessarily reappear in his son, grandson, or more distant descendants.

COLBERT

If an absolute monarch can create about him a group of loyal and efficient ministers with an esprit de corps, or an effective aristocracy which can be perpetuated, through heredity, and thus provide the material for a bureaucracy with coherence and momentum, the efficiency of absolutism may perhaps be transmitted from generation to generation. The very nature of absolutism, however, prevents just this conjunction of factors. As in the case of Louis XIV, the absolute king fears powerful and highly competent men near his throne; he can tolerate none who may become rivals in any fashion, none who may lessen the lustre of his own brilliance. Louis, it is true, inherited from his predecessor a number of able servants who became ministers of signal attainment. He allowed no one of them to rise to independent power or influence; none of them, for example, was ever invested with the title of first minister. High titles, which suggested traditional greatness and former power in the state, were one by one eliminated. No more Grand Admirals of France; no more High Constables; no more Cardinal dukes as first ministers. After the first generation of Louis' best ministers departed, their places were filled by lesser men of no outstanding merits. Some of the earlier, more distinguished ministers we shall note below. In some ways the most important was Jean Baptiste Colbert (1619-1683), who came very near to being a great statesman.

Colbert's service to France was chiefly economic, although he is also to be remembered as a master organizer in the general field of administration, and as a zealous patron of intellectual interests.* He virtually created the modern French navy, and made an important contribution toward the codification of French law. As a financial reformer, however, and as a leader in the development of French industry and commerce, he is chiefly celebrated. He established order in the accounts of the royal revenue, increased the sources of this revenue, and improved the method of its collection. It was the success of these financial measures that made possible the glory of Louis XIV. Without the money which Colbert secured, the effort of France to attain preeminence in Europe could not have been sustained, nor could Versailles have radiated French taste and culture throughout the world. It is possible, also, that without the vigor and impetus which Colbert injected into the royal finance, France could not have averted, until 1789, the inevitable crash of revolution. In encouraging manufactures, protecting them with tariffs and other regulations, introducing new industries, building roads and canals, he gave French life new energy. In supporting trading companies, ship-building, and the development of colonies, he created new

* Cf. L. B. Packard, *The Commercial Revolution*, Ch. II., for a more detailed treatment. (Berkshire Studies, Holt.)

spheres for this energy, and in the navy gave it a protecting force. Had Louis XIV and the nobility appreciated this "offer of Colbert" to make France the richest and most powerful economic state of Europe, it is conceivable that Louis' glory might have been more enduring.

THE DEFECTS OF ABSOLUTE MONARCHY

In its outward show and glamor, the Grand Monarchy was deceptive. By frittering away the income of the state on the superficial brilliance of Versailles, by the corruption of the nobility, and by the policy of endless rivalries with other dynasties, Louis XIV drained France of her strength. The solid and unpretentious triumphs of peace were neglected for the spectacular and bloody feats of diplomacy and arms. Pomp and vanity of a dynasty overwhelmed the substantial, humdrum welfare of the masses of the people. Beneath the surface of courtly splendor and military heroics, the elements of disaster were accumulating. What we call the "abuses" of the Old Régime were becoming increasingly intolerable. The peasants, burdened with a disproportionate share of the taxes, harassed by petty exactions such as salt taxes and other survivals of feudal usage, and humiliating inferiorities; the bourgeoisie, also unjustly taxed, but growing increasingly resentful, more and more stimulated by the ideas of the critics, and less and less willing to submit to the social and political inferiority thrust upon them by the aristocracy; the general inefficiency of the government in alleviating the conditions of these "abuses"; the exemptions and privileges extended to certain classes and officials; the slowness and expense of courts of justice; the petty tyrannies of officials; the obstacles to the free course of trade and industry, such as gilds, tolls, and regulations,—all these defects were present in the government of Louis XIV. Worse, however, than their existence, was the fact that the administration of so great and powerful a monarch made no serious attempt to grapple with them and improve the conditions under which they prevailed. Quite the contrary, monarchy aggravated them with more and more burdens—more wars, more glory, more mistresses and pensions, and, finally, with religious intolerance.

THE REVOCATION OF THE EDICT OF NANTES

Since 1598, when the popular Henry of Navarre (Henry IV) had granted the French Protestants (Huguenots) the right to practice their own religious worship, to have towns and fortresses in which they might guarantee their freedom, and to share in the offices of the state, they had been molested only by Richelieu's attack on their exceptional political privileges. Their fortified towns and other special privileges were taken away, but in their religious affairs they had been reasonably free from persecution. Economically, the Huguenots had prospered; they were particularly active in industry. Mostly of the bourgeois and artisan classes, they were thrifty tradesmen and craftsmen, hard working, and in general, honest and loyal.

They constituted, perhaps, less than 10 per cent of the whole population, but none the less a valuable element.

Their independence in religious matters, however, irked the king. Ardent Catholics, of course, regarded them as heretics, and were always on the look-out for an opportunity to suppress their heresy. In Louis XIV these Catholics found a willing and active supporter. To a monarch who prided himself upon his Divine Right, and especially upon his absolute authority, it was annoying that a section of his subjects should be so irreverent as to think differently upon religious matters from their august and divinely inspired master. Louis was extremely devout and pious, despite his indifference to moral restraints in actual conduct. He was undoubtedly sincere in his detestation of heresy, but his pride was even more touched by the thought of Huguenot non-conformity. It is even possible, moreover, that in favoring an attack upon Huguenot heresy, Louis was urged by other motives. In his last mistress (ultimately his wife), Madame de Maintenon, he found a guide who seriously tried to direct his interests to a better appreciation of religion. It is even possible that he may have felt that operations against heretics would be a sort of penance, a righteous amend for the scandals of his own earlier life. He may also have recalled that he had many times opposed the pope in diplomatic affairs, and a rigorous measure against heretics would be an acceptable make-weight in relations with the Holy Father.

Convinced, at any rate, that Protestantism should be eliminated, and that religious unity was as desirable as political unity, Louis XIV began one of the most serious mistakes of his reign. At first, the Huguenots were deprived of all privileges not directly accorded to them in law; they were excluded from public offices, and many of the professions. Then efforts were made to convert Protestant communities to Catholicism, either by preaching, or by applying the law that children at seven years of age could select their own religion. It was not always difficult, with the suitable inducements, to tempt a child to declare his conversion! Legal penalties could be exacted from parents who interfered with such a conversion. By 1681, came the use of the dragonnades to hasten conversions. This consisted in quartering dragoons, soldiers often of the most brutal and licentious type, upon peaceful Protestant households, exposing them to insult and even crime. Fear of these terrible dragonnades drove many Protestants into at least a superficial conversion. The king and his devout adviser, Madame de Maintenon, were delighted to receive long lists of these conversions. Zealots sought to curry royal favor by submitting such evidences of conformity. Louis was doubtless led to think, before long, that there were few heretics; he knew little, of course, of the horrible details of enforced conversions; he had no means of knowing whether or not the lists of converts submitted to him were genuine. It seemed to him that the few Huguenots remaining dispensed with the necessity of keeping the Edict of Nantes in force as a law. Hence, in 1685, came the revocation of this celebrated edict. After this, no Protestant worship could be legally held in France. Huguenot pastors were banished, and all Protestant churches closed.

At once, it became apparent that by no means all the Huguenots had been converted; hundreds of thousands, it now was revealed, had not conformed to the king's religious views. But nothing was done to remedy the situation. Legally, Protestantism did not exist; its devotees were deprived of the protection of law, and were hounded from one injustice and abuse to another. None were permitted, by law, to leave France. Catholics rejoiced; flatterers congratulated Louis that now, at last, he was king, and told him that this was the greatest act of his reign. The outcome, however, was quite otherwise than great or encouraging. It was necessary to employ the dragonnades more terribly than ever. Many Protestants were imprisoned or sent to living deaths in the galleys, and thousands, in spite of the law, fleeing from this scourge of persecution, sought refuge abroad. Over two hundred thousand, it is estimated, left France, thus taking away some of the most valuable labor, skill, and thrift the nation possessed.

To England, Holland and Brandenburg they went,— even overseas to the English colonies in America, and to the Dutch colony in South Africa. They carried abilities, especially industrial and commercial, and helped not only to develop the economic strength of the potential enemies of France, but also to stimulate fear of Louis XIV, and dread of his religious intolerance.

It is not without significance that in the World War, high officials in the German Army and Navy bore such names as von François and Souchon. Even in France, the persecution did not succeed. Although they lost over half of their numbers, the Huguenots continued in their obstinacy. In the south, particularly, they persisted. As late as 1703 an open revolt of Protestants occurred in the Cévennes, where Huguenots called Camisards, from the shirts (camise) they wore for identification, resisted the royal army itself. In spite of the use of regular troops, the rebels were not subdued, and in the end, the government granted them terms and even pardon. It was not until shortly before the Revolution, in 1789, that they secured, once more, a decent toleration. Protestantism in France survived, and still exists. The present occupant (1929) of the French presidency is M. Doumergue, the first Protestant since Henry IV to reach the chief magistracy.

SUMMARY

By way of summarizing this chapter, we may note that the reign of Louis XIV occurred at the moment when the trend toward absolute monarchy had reached its fullest development. Accepted by the age as a monarchy by Divine Right, it became, in the hands of Louis, completely realized. In his person, in his court at Versailles, in the government of councils, in his policy of aggrandizing his dynasty, Louis exemplified the theories and ideals of absolute monarchy. His diplomatic and military ambitions, in the interest of his dynasty, forced Europe, as we shall see, into combinations against him to preserve the balance of power. The cost of these policies, and his revocation of the Edict of Nantes, helped to undermine the strength and resources of his kingdom, providing, ultimately, for the eighteenth-century trend toward revolution.

CHAPTER II

INTERNATIONAL ASPECTS OF THE REIGN OF LOUIS XIV

THE ADVENT OF MODERN DIPLOMACY

DIPLOMACY may be defined as the art of managing, by negotiations, the intercourse among states, and as the adjustment of their relations. Although it is true that diplomacy has existed since very early times, it did not acquire its full significance until modern states came into existence. This occurred, as we have noted, approximately between 1400 and 1600. It was on the threshold of the Age of Louis XIV that the first formal recognition of the existence of modern states appeared. By the Treaty of Westphalia, in 1648, the new order of Europe's political units, the dynastic states, was definitely and officially established.

Among these new units a new kind of relationship necessarily came about. Antiquity with its various empires or city states, the medieval period with its spiritual dominion of the papacy, its Holy Roman Empire, and its feudalism, all had possessed nothing precisely resembling the dynastic state of the Renaissance and modern times. Both the Roman Empire and its ghostly successor, the Holy Roman Empire, as well as the papacy, were theoretically universal dominions tran-

scending such units as states, and giving no scope to
relations such as those between states. Rivalries and
conflicts were perhaps the first relations of the new
states with one another; there were comparatively few
customs or principles, other than those of war, according to which intercourse between states could be
conducted. By the time of the Treaty of Westphalia,
however, it became apparent that if the states of Europe
were to continue to exist, if they were to avoid destruction through exhausting conflicts, or if they were to
prevent their own absorption by a single conquering
power, they must learn to live, for some of the time, at
peace; war must become the exceptional and not the
normal condition of the continent. Relations must
ordinarily be those of negotiation, and not war. Negotiations must be those of diplomacy, and not of arms.

As a basis for such relations there must naturally be
some generally accepted principles or usages which
could be maintained between states. There must arise
customs or laws which would become international.
The devastating effect of war between the dynastic
states was brought home to Europe by the long struggle
between the Hapsburgs and the Valois (who were ultimately supplanted by the Bourbons, both being
branches of the Capetian dynasty), a struggle, the first
phase of which extended from 1494 to 1559. The
Thirty Years' War (1618-1648) still further ravaged
Europe and drew into its wastage nearly all the states
of the continent. The cruelty and suffering of these
scourges began, at last, to make an impression on the
European mind and first led to attempts to formulate

rules for mitigating the horrors of war. Protection for non-combatants, care for the wounded, and restraint of sacking and pillaging constituted the early efforts. Such needs slowly led to more ambitious attempts at providing rules or general principles for the conduct of states, so that by remaining normally at peace, questions of non-combatants, wounded, sack, and pillage would be less frequently raised.

Significantly enough, the first conspicuous effort of this kind was a treatise published in 1625, during the course of the Thirty Years' War. It was entitled *De Jure Belli ac Pacis* (On the Law of War and Peace). Its author, Hugo Grotius (1583-1645), has come to be acclaimed as the father of International Law. Other men, of course, had prepared the way, as is almost always the case for the advent of epoch-making changes. A Dominican, François de Victoire (d. 1546), and a Jesuit, Francisco Suarez (1548-1617), had set forth thoughtful analyses of human needs transcending the boundaries of states, and of the nature of law between states. Alberico Gentile (1552-1608), a heretic under condemnation of the Inquisition, wrote a treatise called *De Jure Belli,* in which he drew upon both Civil and Canon law to define the laws of war and peace. But higher than both of these authorities, he found in the *Jus Naturæ* (The Law of Nature), the ultimate form of righteousness, the highest common sense of mankind. Nature, or common sense, would hold that peace, and not war should prevail. Gentile grasped, as a whole, the nature of the relations of states to one another, and distinguished these relations as international problems, different from all other legal relationships.

It was the work of Grotius, none the less, which first attracted widespread attention, and exerted a distinct influence upon the subsequent development of international law. He made the first influential attempt to define a principle of right which should govern the relations of states; he sought for a basis for human society outside the Church or the Bible, by establishing it on a foundation of morality and justice. Nature herself provides such a fundamental law, as immutable and true as the very principles which control the existence of the universe itself. The reputation of Grotius' work has been more widespread and more enduring, perhaps, than that ever enjoyed by any other legal treatise.

Somewhat later, in 1672, appeared Pufendorf's *On the Law of Nature and Nations* (Samuel Pufendorf, 1632-1694). This work reinforced the earlier productions of Gentile and Grotius and definitely created a basis among civilized states for new conceptions as to their relations. The true state of Nature, said Pufendorf, is not war, but peace. Peace is indeed feeble and insecure, and must be fortified by law to preserve mankind. International law is not restricted to Christendom, but constitutes a common bond between all nations because all nations form a part of humanity. Wars should be waged only for just motives, and only for defence. Force alone should not regulate the relations of peoples. To observe treaties is the wisest practice, and should be the greatest strength of kings.

To point out that a growth of ideas or principles called international law accompanied the growth of states is not to assert that the states obeyed or even observed this body of law. Far from it. The creation of the states, as we have observed, was largely a process of force, by which kings subjected vassals and neighbors, and thus conquered their kingdoms. It was not strange, then, that in their relations with other kingdoms, kings, for a long time, employed chiefly force, sometimes tempered with guile, in seeking their ends. Among early modern states relations were, as among the political units of antiquity, normally relations of hostility. Force, that is war, was the principal medium of these relations. It was not surprising, therefore, that a long time elapsed before kings were much influenced by legal treatises or theories of international law. It was a long time before wisdom, common sense, and a notion of justice led them to seek to establish a basis of law for the relations of state with state, as there had for a considerable period been a basis of law for the relations of man with man. From the time of the Treaty of Westphalia, however, the importance of this trend steadily increased. There were numerous discouraging setbacks, but no permanent cessation. "Before the law," says an eminent international lawyer of the present day, "all men are equal; before the law all states are equal. In the domain of justice there is neither large nor small, powerful nor weak. There are only equals in rights, equals in duty, and the rights and duties are not determined of the sword, but weighed in the balance of justice."

It is toward the full realization of this aim of international law that diplomacy has striven, and still strives. The end is by no means attained, but there is a goal. Among the first diplomatic steps there was much that was crude, unjust, and dishonest. Early modern diplomacy was still close to the time when force was almost the only form of adjusting the relations of states. Only very gingerly and hesitatingly did states trust to the offices of diplomacy. The duties of a diplomatic agent or an ambassador were at first regarded practically as those of a military spy. A regular, permanent system of diplomatic representation came slowly into existence. In antiquity and during the Middle Ages agents were employed between political powers primarily for particular missions or on specific occasions. The medieval papacy was perhaps the first to begin the practice of sending semi-permanent agents to reside with the various European political authorities and represent papal interests. They were termed legates, and later, nuncios.

In the later Middle Ages, when the city states of Italy began to emerge as political powers, their relations with one another rendered imperative a more or less systematic intercourse. By the thirteenth century a number of these states had developed in northern and central Italy; in many ways they were precursors of the later, larger dynastic states. They were constantly fighting with one another for territory, for political supremacy, or for economic advantages. They made alliances, established a kind of balance of power to prevent the domination of any one city, and they developed among themselves the elements of the diplomacy which was subsequently to become international. They devised a system of embassies, of passports, and a body of customs and principles which strongly affected the later growth of international law. They came to the realization, as the greater states ultimately did, that law, the observance of principles and forms of comity, were as necessary among city states as among individual men.

Among the ambassadors who served these city states were such men as Dante, Petrarch, and Boccaccio. Later, Machiavelli became active in diplomacy, both in theory and practice. It was in Venice, particularly, that the beginnings of systematic diplomacy occurred. Her far-flung commercial undertakings, and her financial interests in so many lands led the Queen of the Adriatic to organize a regular diplomatic service. Byzantine influence, encountered at Constantinople, may have furnished the stimulus and ideas which led to Venetian developments in diplomacy. Following the thirteenth century, Venice created a body of rules for the guidance of her diplomatic agents, and produced a remarkably well-trained and skillful group of ambassadors. The full and generally accurate reports of these ambassadors have survived and may be studied in detail. At first, ambassadors were sent out for short terms only. For a long time, they were regarded by governments to whom they were sent, with deep suspicion, and were viewed as spies sent to watch the military strength of the state and its military policy. Gradually, however, it became apparent that their services were much more comprehensive than the gathering of information about things military. The first permanent embassy was perhaps that sent by the Sforza duke of Milan, in 1455, to represent him at Genoa. Within a few years, many other states established the practice of permanent ambassadors or envoys.

Almost from the beginning, the conduct and policy of ambassadors were associated with secrecy, dishonesty, and trickery. Not only were they suspected of spying, but they were also supposed to be charged with deceiving governments to which they were accredited, and with the duty of winning advantages for their own countries by fair means or foul. The often repeated statement of Sir Henry Wotton, an English ambassador of the seventeenth century, that an ambassador was an honest man sent to lie abroad for the good of his country, expresses a still popular conception. It is only fair to Sir Henry, however, to observe that he was guilty of committing a pun, for his use of the verb *lie* could, in the usage of the seventeenth century, be also interpreted as equivalent to the word *reside*. Much of this evil reputation of diplomacy was derived from Machiavelli's discussions of ambassadors and their duties.

With his perfect frankness and somewhat cynical regard for means, Machiavelli expounded his ideas of how states should conduct their relations in order to secure a maximum of success. To be strong, and to be in a position to secure advantages for the welfare and defence of the state constituted the aims of his diplo-

macy. With him, results very decidedly overshadowed
the means. His name, consequently, though not wholly
with justice, became associated with unscrupulous and
treacherous conduct. All or any diplomacy came to
be described as Machiavellian. With the practice of
Italian diplomacy as a model, such keen and crafty
kings as Louis XI of France (1461-1483), Henry VII
of England (1485-1509), and Ferdinand and Isabella
of Spain (1474-1516) laid the foundations of state
diplomacy. In view of the character and ambitions of
these monarchs, it is not at all strange that Machiavellian, in its worst sense, should be the adjective
attached to diplomacy. Louis XI is reported, for instance, to have said to two of his ambassadors depart-
ing on a mission, "If they lie to you, you lie still
more to them." Of Ferdinand of Spain it is said that,
when he heard that his neighbor, Louis XII of France
had declared, "This is the second time Ferdinand has
deceived me," he remarked, "Louis lies, it is the twelfth
time I have deceived him."

DIPLOMACY IN THE AGE OF LOUIS XIV

In no respect is the preeminence of France during the
seventeenth century more clearly to be seen than in the
effect which Louis XIV and his policy exerted upon the
development of diplomacy. One of the first requisites
of communications between states is a medium of expression, i.e., a language. Latin had been the international language on the eve of the appearance of the
modern states, but with the Renaissance, vernacular

speech and literature gradually replaced Latin. Diplomacy began to be practiced contemporaneously with the rise of France to European prominence. The French language moreover, was at the same time acquiring a wide reputation for its inherent excellence, and for the literature in which it was embodied. The king of France was practicing diplomacy in a grand and masterly fashion. French interests were actively manifested all over the world, and the French language became, during the seventeenth century, indisputably the most widespread and most frequently used of any of the modern languages. French became, consequently, the language most extensively used in communication between states. It became, par excellence, the language of diplomacy. Its precision, clarity and elegance, its polish and scientific exactness fitted it admirably for use in diplomatic documents, above all for use in treaties where a perfect understanding and absence of ambiguity are always necessary. As such it has remained virtually unchallenged until the twentieth century. With the recent expansion of the English-speaking world, and the political and economic importance of the English-speaking states, English has assumed a position of at least equality in diplomatic exchanges. For the first time, in general modern treaty-making, an English text takes its place alongside the French as official, in the Treaty of Versailles (1920).

As the France of Louis XIV thus supplied a language for diplomacy, so the policy and influence of her monarch provided a pattern and a fashion for the conduct

of diplomacy. "The seventeenth is the great century
of French diplomacy. Never did the diplomats of the
Most Christian King exercise greater prestige, hold a
firmer or more vigorous tone; never did they display
greater skill. Their activity was incomparable. Their
rôle was of the first rank. They were charged with
the negotiation of princely alliances, with the task of
making partition treaties. In an age when states were
considered as the patrimony of reigning families, when
the fate of peoples was regulated by the convenience
of sovereigns, without even consulting their subjects,
the diplomats had in their hands, even more, perhaps,
than the military men, the destinies of history." These
diplomats in the service of Louis XIV were of two general kinds. First, there were the great nobles whose
functions were purely ceremonial. Dukes, counts, and
marshals would be sent on missions to represent the
king in paying formal visits, and in conveying royal
sentiments. Secondly, there was the much more important group of envoys who were sent to reside at
other courts.

These men were usually lawyers or administrative
officials of experience who could be depended upon to
carry out their instructions effectively, intelligently, and
faithfully. They were furnished with instructions by
the king or his secretaries, and were expected to report
in extensive correspondence, and in every detail to look
after the interests of France. One of their heaviest
duties was to remedy the mistakes made by the more
exalted and ornamental diplomats. Generally speaking, the diplomatic instructions which were given them

were definite and compact, leaving them considerable latitude. They were entrusted with initiative and responsibility. Many difficulties beset them, however; the uncertain means of communication and the delays in time; exposure to intrigues and interference with the mails and despatches; they were constantly spied upon. To accomplish their ends, they could not be overscrupulous; they must use spying, themselves, and bribery was regularly expected of them. For the latter purpose, "secret service" funds were placed at their disposal. Frequently, French agents as well as those of other countries, bought and sold votes in the electoral body which chose the Holy Roman Emperor. Most of the German states, in fact, were notorious as a field for diplomatic bribery. No one could resist the seduction of French money. "Little princes incessantly held out their hands, the greater princes their hats."

French interests were so extensive and French prestige was so exalted that the manifold activities of Louis XIV required a numerous diplomatic staff. A tradition of excellence in this service was built up which not only furnished France with trained men, but which also gave all the European states a model. Louis, himself, as we have seen, was a diplomat of the first rank, possessing preeminently the qualities which are set down as most necessary. Smooth and attractive manners, shrewdness, and the art of using personal influence in managing men, becoming dress, polish, dignity, and tact were peculiarly associated with Louis XIV. Inasmuch as these qualities were commonly acquired at court, Versailles was an effective training school. The tone of the profession was decidedly aristocratic and few monarchs could excel Louis in imparting such a tone.

What set this seal upon French leadership in diplomacy, and profoundly impressed other kings and peoples, was not only the strength of France, the pride and dazzling magnificence of her king, but also the determination of Louis to enforce respect for, and acknowledgment of, his position. From the moment of his assumption of control of the government, he announced that in important matters he would himself deal with the diplomatic representatives of France. He thus acquired a remarkable knowledge of diplomatic affairs, "learning Europe by heart, the strength of its states, the secrets of its courts, and every detail of significance." He demanded of other states that his diplomatic agents be regarded as his personal representatives and that, as deputies of the Sun King, they be accorded precedence over all other diplomats.

When the Baron de Watteville, Spanish ambassador to King Charles II of England, ventured, in 1661, to assert his precedence to the Count d'Estrades, ambassador of Louis XIV, all Europe was startled by the results. The Spaniard determined to place his coach first, after that of King Charles, in a court procession moving to greet a newly arrived ambassador from Sweden; he employed armed retainers who killed the horses of the French envoy and dispersed the French guard, forcing the Count d'Estrades entirely out of the procession. Louis learned of this affront five days

later. His anger was magnificent. He ordered the
Spanish ambassador at Versailles to leave France, and
informed the king of Spain that he must punish the
Baron de Watteville, and also instruct all of his envoys
that, henceforth, Spanish ambassadors in every court
of Europe must give precedence to those of France.
A formal apology, moreover, must be made by a high
official of Spain, in person, to the king of France.   In
face of the obvious intention of Louis XIV to enforce
these demands, by war if necessary, Spain could only
yield.   The Baron de Watteville was punished, all
Spanish ambassadors were ordered to concede precedence to those of Louis, and the humble apology was
sent to Versailles.   Louis assembled all the foreign
envoys, the princes of the blood, the officials of the
state, and all other "persons of quality" to witness the
presentation.   Thus did Europe learn of the triumph
of the Grand Monarch, and thus was established the
prestige and preeminence of France.

A short time afterwards, in 1662, Louis again asserted the importance of France. He challenged that
naval practice of England which expected that ships
of all nations meeting the English flag in the "seas of
England" should salute first.   Charles II yielded, and
ordered that on the Atlantic and in the Mediterranean,
his flag should salute "equally" with that of France,
and also that even in English waters, his ships should
avoid the exaction of the first salute.

Not even the pope, in his exalted position, was to
escape the determined assertion of French preeminence. Once more, in 1662, occurred an incident; this

time at Rome. It was a brawl between the Corsican guard of the pope and three drunken Frenchmen. Shots were fired at the palace of the French ambassador to the Vatican. One of the ambassador's pages was killed. No punishment, however, was inflicted upon the Corsican guard, and the pope was slow to express his regrets for what had happened. Louis XIV at once recalled his envoy and informed the pope, in very haughty language, that he would exact vengeance for such a barbarous outrage. Louis' intention was characteristic of certain phases of diplomacy; he expected to frighten the pope into a humiliating apology, thus cheaply gaining prestige and glory—an aim only too frequent in diplomacy. In order to give point to his intentions, Louis allowed the annexation to France of two papal possessions on the Rhone, Avignon and the Comtat Venaissin. Some 3,500 soldiers were also started on the way to Italy. The pope had hoped to find protection by forming a combination of various powers against France into a sort of Holy League. He met with little success, and was ultimately forced to yield to Louis. The king returned the annexed papal territories, but the pope had to send his nephew, the Cardinal Chigi, to Versailles, who there, in the full publicity of all Europe, presented the pope's apologies. His Holiness was then compelled to disband his Corsican guard, and to erect a stone pyramid in Rome bearing an inscription, "in large and well designed letters" commemorating the papal excuses. The reparation thus made, far exceeded, of course, the original injury; it served, however, to glorify Louis XIV, to enhance his diplomacy, and to create a general European effect.

It should be noted that the accumulation of national prestige by such diplomatic maneuvers, as in these incidents cited from Louis' policy, became one of the recognized aims of diplomacy. Prestige of this sort could be used to real advantage in negotiations with other states and often led to substantial, material gains. Such diplomacy, however, naturally became dangerous; it was a kind of international bullying, and eventually tended to produce animosities and resentment. An atmosphere of distrust and hostility came inevitably to surround the conduct of many a negotiation which should have been based upon mutual confidence and respect. It was unfortunate that diplomacy, supposedly devoted to the adjustment of international difficulties, should come, by reason of its affection for prestige, under the suspicion of increasing rather than decreasing these difficulties.

Another expression of Louis' search for diplomatic effect occurred in the elaborate exchange of embassies between France and Siam. In 1680, as a factor in the commercial rivalry with the English and the Dutch in the East, France endeavored to cultivate relations with Siam. Every attempt was made, at Versailles, to dazzle the Siamese ambassadors with the splendor and magnificence of Louis XIV, his court, and his resources.

With the reputation thus developed by Louis XIV for diplomatic firmness, if not for unparalleled arrogance, the whole continent could not but stand in awe of the French king. It is not to be wondered at, furthermore, that when Louis began to apply his diplomacy to increasing French power and French territory at the expense of other dynastic states, this awe should turn into fear, and eventually weld most of Europe together into resistance against French pretensions and aggression.

THE BEGINNINGS OF MODERN MILITARISM—THE FIRST GREAT STANDING ARMY

Most effective in giving point to the diplomacy of Louis XIV, and in creating throughout Europe a dread of French power, was the huge military machine constructed during the reign of "le grand monarque." This, the first of the colossal modern military establishments, was by no means a sudden innovation. It was preceded by the long history of the art of war to which man has, from the earliest times, devoted some of his best intellectual effort, and much of his energy. However strongly we may deplore this fact, or however much we may, in this twentieth century, be opposed to the use of war as a means of international adjustment, we should not, from the historical point of view, overlook the influence which warfare has exerted in times past. What we may now believe, or favor, has no influence upon the facts of the past. Because we may not believe, to-day, in what we call militarism, does not justify us in ignoring the great effect which military activities have exerted in history. It is perhaps true that historical writing of an earlier date dwelt too exclusively upon wars, battles, and peace treaties, upon what is now called "drum and trumpet history." This is no reason, however, for rushing to the other extreme, and ignoring them entirely. Such would not be properly historical, any more than it is correctly historical to say that we must discourage militarism by avoiding all reference to everything in the past associated with things military.

It is the historian's duty to try to determine fact and, in interpreting fact, to try to discern what influence it exerted; this he must do regardless of prejudice, favor or disfavor, and without reference to what may or may not be the interest of his own generation. The art (or science) of war and affairs military have played an enormous rôle in the history of European civilization, from antiquity to our own day. Too much of a rôle undoubtedly, according to our present ideas, but we cannot shirk the obligation of seeing this rôle in the setting of its own day, and trying to estimate its nature and importance.

With the decline of feudalism and the growth of the state, military institutions, and also the conduct of war, took on a new character and importance. During the sixteenth century, military effort began to assume an organization and system unknown in the days of feudal irregularity and independence. When Charles VIII of France invaded Italy, in 1494, his troops constituted a force more carefully equipped and controlled, perhaps, than any similar body of soldiers since the days of Byzantine military greatness. It was an army, of sorts. The campaigns in Italy which followed the French invasion saw the rise to power of the famous

Spanish infantry under the "Great Captain," Gonsalvo de Cordova. This rise was based not only on the skillful leadership of Gonsalvo, but also on the effective organization of the Spanish troops. Subsequent conflicts between France and Spain, during the latter part of the sixteenth century, saw the Spanish military system operating in the Netherlands, where Maurice of Nassau further contributed to the art of warfare by developing drill and discipline. His ideas were inspired by a study of Roman methods.

In the first part of the following century, from 1618 to 1648, came the Thirty Years' War. In this devastating struggle, the organizing genius of Gustavus Adolphus of Sweden carried the manipulation and equipment of his troops still further toward the standard of a modern army. In both tactics and matériel Gustavus was an innovator of the first order. He secured greater mobility in his formations and movements, and he improved his weapons by producing a lighter musket, cartridges, and less clumsy field pieces for his artillery. In the handling of cavalry, Gustavus recovered the use of shock tactics, so successfully employed later by Oliver Cromwell. He also developed discipline, and a system of supply far more regular and effective in the subsistence of troops than pillaging.

In France, the way for the armies of Louis XIV was prepared by the indefatigable Richelieu. Borrowing from Swedish ideas, and actually taking into French service some of the remnants of the army of Gustavus, Richelieu provided for new foundations for the French military system. Taught by one of Gustavus' lieutenants (Bernard of Saxe-Weimar), Turenne, a young French officer, rose to be perhaps the greatest French soldier before the time of Napoleon. Under Richelieu, organization was improved, infantry began to occupy a place of importance with the cavalry, and, above all, a more effective system of command was arranged. Richelieu instituted a department of State for the management of military matters, i.e., a ministry of war, with military intendants who centralized more thoroughly than ever the conduct of the army and its activities. He abolished the office of Constable of France, a rank and title so exalted that its exercise had formerly menaced even the power of the crown, and established a gradation of military offices and titles.

From these improvements which have been mentioned in connection with the names of Gonsalvo, Maurice, Gustavus, and Richelieu, it must not be supposed that we have yet reached the army in its modern sense. Even the forces led by Turenne in the last days of Richelieu were far different from the present conception of an organized fighting army. The "armies" of these earlier days were but loose assemblages of units, some of which might be reasonably well trained, others might be of the militia type of citizen soldiers, and still others might be groups of professional adventurers, particularly Swiss or German mercenaries. There was almost no system of higher command, but only an irregular arrangement of officers serving under the personal authority of some general or group of generals. Most of the officers, both high

and low, were nobles, many of whom had had little
military training and possessed no sense of discipline
or cooperation, their personal bravery alone qualifying
them for leadership. Their intense and highly sensitive
pride, their irregularities, indiscipline, and independence were still a strong and living inheritance from
feudal days.

Of the commissions below the grade of general officers, most were purchased, and the enlisted personnel
was recruited on an irregular, irresponsible and un-
official financial basis. Both officers and soldiers were
not, for the most part, on a permanent standing. Nearly
every king, it is true, had created what were called
"standing armies"—the latter had, in fact, been instruments in the destruction of feudal power and in the
establishment of the state. Such armies, however, were
small, consisting of perhaps two or three thousand
soldiers, mostly mercenaries and not very thoroughly
organized. When a war occurred, or a definite expe-
dition was to be made, these troops would be increased
by various means; but such forces existed only for the
specific purpose, and were not maintained as a permanent establishment. Even when enlarged in war
time, these "armies" were comparatively small, including perhaps as many as forty to fifty thousand men.

Before the seventeenth century no common practice
existed as to the arrangement of troops in units.
Regiments, battalions, and companies were terms which
had no fixed status; formations for both tactical, i.e.,
combat purposes and for administrative needs had not
yet attained a recognized usage. Larger combinations,

brigades, divisions, corps, and armies were yet to come. Various branches of the service, such as infantry, cavalry, artillery, and engineers were just beginning to be recognized in the sixteenth century. Cavalry was still adorned with the éclat which it had possessed since feudal times; infantry was slowly assuming greater importance. Engineers were not yet taken seriously and had no recognition as an integral part of an army. Artillery was treated, by the French at least, as hardly belonging to the army at all; it was provided, transported, and even fought by private contractors.

To create a large force of well over one hundred thousand officers and soldiers, maintain it as a permanent, peace-time establishment, officer and train it, provide for its expansion to twice this size, or more, in time of war, arrange it in units of definite status with due regard for the various branches of service, and finally to supply it with munitions and subsistence, in other words, to create a modern army, was an achievement of the Age of Louis XIV. The king himself was keenly interested in this work; he gloried in his reputation as a soldier and in the victories won by his armies. Yet he rarely assumed the command of his troops. He was no strategist, nor did he engage in combat. It is possible that his pride dreaded the loss of prestige entailed in associating his name with reverse or defeat. He was by no means a coward, but he hesitated to risk the chance of a defeat, with which his command could be personally associated. He delighted in reviewing troops; he frequently took the field and established his camps in the vicinity of sieges.

In a siege he rejoiced. As conducted by the incomparable Vauban it was certain to be victorious, and Louis could participate gloriously in the formal entrance into a conquered city. Rarely, however, was the king in military uniform; much as he enjoyed manifestations in honor of the triumph of his arms, he was never merely a military man; he was always, in the fullest sense, the king.

LOUVOIS

To Louvois and Vauban belongs the credit for the creation of the vast military organization of Louis XIV; to Turenne, the merit of unusual excellence in the use of this formidable weapon. François Michel le Tellier, Marquis de Louvois, was the son of one of Louis' secretaries of State, and from the age of fifteen was carefully trained in the art of administration; in this he developed a zeal and competence equal to that of Colbert. In 1666, he became Minister of War, and as such was the only rival of Colbert in the confidence of the king. Like Colbert, he was a bitter enemy of waste and inefficiency; he was eminently a man of honor and probity, but he was cold, brutal, violent, and harsh. He lacked the courage of Colbert in opposing Louis in matters of extravagance, and he was willing, for the sake of gaining what he needed for the army, to flatter and cringe to the king. Thus he eventually gained more influence than his rival. He knew the army, not only from the desk of an administrator, but also from the field, having served an apprenticeship under Turenne.

Louvois found the army neither permanent nor regular. It was recruited, as the taxes were collected, by farming. That is, the Minister of War sold the commissions of the two most important administrative grades, those of colonel and captain. The colonels and captains, in turn, employed recruiting sergeants, who by any means whatever, sought to procure recruits; they got men to enlist while drunk; they got them at any age, with almost any physical defects; they got them by any form of alluring promise as to pay and privileges. Colonels sold commissions for the subaltern officers. Captains were allowed by the War Ministry, for the maintenance and pay of their companies, certain sums based upon the number of soldiers on the company rosters. Scandalous abuses existed, however, so that captains often drew funds for the upkeep of a full company, whereas there might be less than half of the full complement of men actually with the colors. When an inspection occurred, "fillers" (passe volants) would be hired for the day from any available source, and put in line to deceive the inspectors. There was no regular system of training. Most of the troops had no regular uniform; certain units of Royal Guards wore special trappings, and sometimes a unit might wear the livery belonging to the household service of their commander. Discipline was almost non-existent. Officers, being noble, resented taking orders or conforming to regulations. Pillage was ordinarily allowed to troops on campaign.

In weapons, the armies of Europe were undergoing marked changes, among which the most important was the transition from the use of pikes (15 to 20 feet in length), lances, and swords, interspersed with fire-arms, to an almost general employment of firearms. Armor was disappearing and survived chiefly for display, as it still does in the cuirass of some cavalry regiments. Pikes or spears had been used to offer a defence against cavalry charge, and as a protection for slow firing musketeers, and for swordsmen. To move an infantry unit, with its closely packed pikemen, near enough to an enemy for effective fire or sword work, was one of the chief problems of military skill before the innovations of which we are speaking.

In the conduct of warfare, there was still much more of tactics than of strategy. Tactics refers to the conduct of troops in the presence of the enemy, i.e., the actual manipulation of forces in preparing for action and in actual combat. Strategy has to do with the manœuvering of forces before direct contact with the enemy has been attained. As in the times of feudalism, there was still much campaigning, and many sieges, but few pitched battles. A costly engagement, even though a victory, was to be avoided by the successful general. "The ideal campaign was one in which an invader outmanœuvered the defending army, while one fortress after another would be besieged and captured. Fortresses were considered the chief military objectives." In strategy, the preliminary planning and working out of a campaign on a grand scale, lay much of the development to come. In all that lies behind strategy, organization, equipment, training, and in tactics we find the elements of what may be called the science of warfare.

It was Turenne, working with the weapons forged by Louvois, who contributed notably to the development of strategy. Henri de la Tour d'Auvergne, Viscount de Turenne and Marshal of France (1611-1675), was probably the ablest soldier in Europe between the days of Gustavus Adolphus and Frederick the Great, and certainly the greatest French military name after that of Napoleon. He executed with splendid boldness, plans which had been carefully worked out in advance. In scientific military methods he has been called the intellectual precursor of Von Moltke the elder and Ferdinand Foch. He knew the value of speed in movement and, unlike most of his contemporaries, he was not afraid to seek decisive engagements.

With Turenne might also be mentioned a celebrated general of Louis XIV, who was rather a brilliant winner of victories than a systematic contributor to the science of war. This was Louis de Bourbon, Prince de Condé —the Great Condé (1621-1686). At the age of twenty-two, Condé, facing the most renowned troops in Europe, the Spanish infantry, utterly defeated them at Rocroi (1643), and thus ended the long military supremacy of Spain, and inaugurated the reign of French military glory. More versatile than Turenne, he "possessed a power of quick decision and energy, unknown until the eruption of Napoleon into the placid course of chess-like war."

Continuing the work of Richelieu, Louvois began

the construction of a regular military administration, foreshadowing what was much later to become a General Staff. He divided the functions of controlling the army into sections for administration, subsistence (supply), munitions, and inspection. He instituted commissions for dealing with arsenals, transportation, food, remounts for cavalry, hospitals and ambulances, and, above all, for the maintenance of great depôts of supplies. He dealt also with the important problem of field command, making the first systematic arrangement for gradations of higher officials according to rank, as, for example, marshals, lieutenant-generals, generals of brigades, etc. His "ordre de tableau" (order of seniority) introduced a necessary regulation of authority. This produced a concentration of control, and "brought the army back to the king."

Discipline for officers as well as for men was exacted. Noble officers resented this, and hated Louvois as they hated Colbert, because he "had humbled men born to command others on the pretext that it was reasonable to learn to obey before being placed in command." A conversation between Louvois and an officer reveals how the Minister expected even nobles to perform their duties:

LOUVOIS (*very loudly to* M. DE NOGARET): Sir, your company is in a very bad state.
NOGARET: Sir, I was not aware of it.
LOUVOIS: You ought to know it. Have you seen it?
NOGARET: No, sir.
LOUVOIS: You must see it, sir.
NOGARET: I will give an order, sir.

LOUVOIS: It must be given; for, sir, you must decide whether you will be a courtier or an officer, and do your duty as such.

Louvois made an attempt to fix and regularize the units of the army, and to coordinate the various branches of the service. He made the artillery a part of the army, and on the basis of Vauban's work, he instituted a regular engineer corps. Companies, battalions, and regiments began, under his control, to have some permanence and some significance. The practice of grouping regiments into brigades was introduced, and something like system came to the ordering of large bodies of troops. Louvois encouraged the study of the proper coordination of cavalry, infantry, and artillery. He also made efforts to provide a uniform for the whole army, thus creating an important element in discipline. This was the first modern attempt to clothe a large army uniformly. Special designations and insignia were given certain units, thus helping to create the supremely important esprit de corps. Marching in step was introduced; and Louvois provided systematic training in artillery schools at Douai, Metz and Strassburg. "Crack" infantry regiments were organized as models for the rest of the army, and the French infantry rapidly supplanted the Spanish as the most formidable in the world.

With the abuses of privilege, in the army, particularly in the sale of commissions, Louvois had no better luck than Colbert with the financial abuses. He was unable to eliminate them, but he restricted the sale to commissions for colonels and captains; and to these offices he succeeded in attaching carefully trained and experienced deputies, lieutenant-colonels and lieutenants, respectively (offices remaining to the present day), who could really perform the duties of the office. Inspectors were appointed to keep standards high. Among these was the universally known Colonel Martinet, whose reputation for strictness and severity has made his name a synonym for military rigor. Martinet, incidentally, who was Inspector-General for infantry, was the creator of the model regiment known as the King's Regiment.

Equipment was greatly improved. Muskets rapidly replaced pikes, which had practically disappeared by 1703, and hand grenades appeared. The bayonet was perfected (by Vauban, it is said) to enable the musket to be used as a pike, i.e., for repelling cavalry charges. Bayonets had been employed earlier to enable the slow firing musketeers to defend themselves against cavalry, but they had the drawback that it was necessary to fit them into the muzzle of the musket. Vauban found a device which permitted the bayonet to be fixed, on an offset, without preventing the firing of the piece. The types of artillery were reduced in number so that the sizes of projectiles would be fewer, simpler to supply, and more readily available for a greater number of guns. A more general system of barracks for housing troops began to replace the irritating and irregular habit of billeting soldiers in the houses of private individuals. For old soldiers the Hôtel des Invalides was built in Paris, where, as the site of the chapel containing the tomb of Napoleon it is a center of pilgrimage for countless thousands. The Invalides is still a refuge for sick and aged veterans, and also contains a vast military museum.

No remarkable innovations in the conduct of fighting occurred during this period, but the importance of strategy was recognized, and Louvois' institution of a system of planning campaigns was important. Associated with the king and Louvois in organizing campaigns was an expert topographer, the Marquis de Chamlay, who was the chief operations officer of the army. His knowledge of maps and road reports was so extensive that one of the marshals called him a "living map." This board of strategy, the king, Louvois, and Chamlay, worked out precise instructions for their field commanders, giving unity and direction to military undertakings. Such a system had its limitations with all except the greatest generals, but it at least served to furnish a basis for an orderly and scientific study of the problems of war.

As a result of this work of Louvois and his associates, France was enabled to maintain, even in peace times, a professional, standing army of well over 100,-000 men, a huge increase over anything of the sort hitherto attempted by the modern state. Its size introduced one of the problems which has confronted the world ever since: the problem of armament. Payment for such an institution, the burden of armament, the influence wielded by interests bound up in, and dependent upon, such a great system, i.e., its officials, and the contractors who supply it with clothing, food, weapons, and munitions, its effect upon the life of a community through the service of its citizens in the ranks, and through popular pride in its achievements, the power it places in the hands of government, and, finally, the fear and suspicion which it arouses in the governments and peoples of neighboring states,—all these, combine to form the problem of militarism. Of Louis' army, all Europe certainly stood in awe, if not in fear and dread. No other king in Europe had anything equal to this mighty machine of war.

VAUBAN

Inseparably associated with the achievements of Louvois was the work of Vauban. This engineer, Sébastien Le Prestre de Vauban (1633-1707), Marquis and Marshal of France, was of humble birth, and served as a youth under the Great Condé. He devoted much study to mathematics and engineering, and before he was twenty-five, had made a reputation in the conduct of sieges. His skill in this work was soon matched by his ability to construct fortifications. In a day when artillery was still of short range and limited destructive power, the art, or science, of taking and defending fortresses retained some of its medieval significance. Rating only as a captain in the army, Vauban labored many years before he became almost indispensable to the king. Louis' interest in sieges eventually led to the recognition and promotion of Vauban, and the creation of a regular corps of engineers. It was commonly said of Vauban that a city besieged by him was a city captured, and that a city fortified by Vauban was impregnable. It is calculated that his military record included the re-fortification of three hundred fortified towns, the construction of thirty-two new fortresses, and the conduct of fifty-three sieges. Most of the seacoast towns of France were fortified by him.

For the land protection of France, he established two great lines of defence, consisting of the fortification of strategic towns. In his sieges, he developed the use of shells to destroy earthworks; he employed ricochet fire to dismount the defender's guns; and he invented a system of "parallels," i.e., of trenches, projected from the besieger's lines, at angles with the walls of the defence, and approaching them in such wise that the defenders found it practically impossible to check their advance. Many of Vauban's fortifications retained their importance down to the nineteenth century, when long-range guns and high-powered explosive rendered them useless. Incidentally, Vauban was more than a military engineer. He wrote many treatises on siege warfare and the technique of military engineering; his intelligence and general interest in the problems of government and the welfare of his country, led him to think and write on other subjects. His criticism of the abuses of the government, and his suggestions for reform, particularly in taxation, led him out of the king's favor. The sharp-tongued S. Simon honored him with the title of "patriot."

Other states of Europe soon began to pattern their military establishments on the French model. In organization, equipment, and military terminology,

French influence was dominant. Not long after the death of Louis XIV, the Prussian king, Frederick William I, began the development of a similar machine which was to retain its traditions and importance down to 1918.

INTERNATIONAL RELATIONS DURING THE AGE OF LOUIS XIV

To what end was the diplomacy of the Sun King directed? To what purposes was his powerful army directed? Answers to these questions may be very complex, or relatively simple. If we enter upon a detailed examination of the diplomatic combinations, intrigues, partition treaties, and other international relations of the period from 1661 to 1715, we shall find a veritable maze, wherein it is difficult to follow the main threads of the historical strand. If, however, we observe the general status of the countries of Europe at this time, and then ask what their governments were trying to do, particularly what Louis XIV was trying to do in connection with these states, we shall discern certain outstanding, comparatively simple factors.

Aside from France, the principal states of Europe in the Age of Louis XIV may be listed, and their interests summarized somewhat as follows:

England, with a restored Stuart monarchy, trying under Charles II, (1660-1685), to consolidate the royal power, foster Catholic interests, and protect a rapidly growing commerce; trying under James II (1685-1688) to make the royal power absolute, to reintroduce Catholicism, and, for assistance against Parliament and the Protestants, depending upon the financial and diplomatic support of Louis XIV. Finally, in 1688, the English overthrew James II, and his royal pretensions to absolute power, accepted Parliamentary supremacy, made the Dutch William III king, and joined the general European opposition to the ambitions of Louis XIV for continental supremacy.

Spain, under the decrepit, elder branch of the House of Hapsburg, gradually losing her strength, but holding tenaciously to her prestige and possessions in Italy, the Franche-Comté, and the southern Netherlands; confronted with the prospect of seeing her dominions, at the death of King Charles II, the last of the Spanish Hapsburgs, partitioned by her vigorous and more powerful neighbors; striving to maintain her colonial and commercial interests in the face of growing Dutch and English competition.

The Hapsburg Monarchy, controlling Austria and portions of northern Italy, possessing the elective title of Holy Roman Emperor, which gave the Hapsburgs a presidency, but no effective control, over the German states, confronted with the menace of a new wave of Turkish invasion, led by the vigorous Ottoman vizirs, the Kiuprilis; hoping to repel this invasion, and recover the land of Hungary, and the territories of the Slavs adjacent to the Danube valley. To the menace of the Turks was added that of Transylvania, whose active and intriguing princes played now with the Hungarians, and now with the Sultans. The second half of the seventeenth century has been described as the most critical in the history of the Hapsburgs.

The German States of the Holy Roman Empire, several hundred in number, but ranging in size from the most important such as Brandenburg-Prussia, Saxony, Bavaria, and the Hesses, through the smaller ecclesiastical states, down to the diminutive principalities which were mere specks on the map, being actually no larger than a good-sized American township. Devastated and weakened by the Thirty Years' War, their virtual independence conceded by the Treaty of Westphalia, these states were constantly seeking protection against the authority of the Hapsburg emperors, and against the growing strength and ambitions of some of their own number, particularly Brandenburg-Prussia and Bavaria. Of these, the former, under Frederick William, the Great Elector (1640-1688), was becoming an "absolutist" state, and laying the foundations of great economic and military prowess.

The Scandinavian States (Sweden and Denmark-Norway), both declining from an earlier position of much power, still taking advantage of the lack of unity among the German states, to play a German rôle, interested in the commerce and navigation of the Baltic, jealous of Poland, and already aroused by the increasing strength and ambitions of Russia. Sweden, but recently (1630-1635) the most powerful military state on the continent, became dependent upon France for financial support; nevertheless, under her brilliant military king, Charles XII, she played an important part in the Great Northern War among the Baltic states. Denmark-Norway became in the period 1660-1670 an Absolute Monarchy.

Poland, a poorly centralized, weakly governed state, situated on the map of Europe at a place where the ambitions of Sweden, the German states, the Hapsburgs, the Russians, and the Turks conflicted. Her monarchy was an elective kingship which afforded opportunity, at each election, for foreign governments to intervene and play politics.

Russia (recently known as Muscovy), a partly civilized state, on the point of coming under the ambitious and powerful leadership of Peter the Great (1695-1725), whose aim was to carry Russian boundaries to the sea, through Swedish, Polish, or Turkish territory; to make Russia a European power, and to introduce occidental civilization.

The Ottoman Empire, an Asiatic-European state, controlling Constantinople, the Black Sea, the lower Danube, and the Balkan peninsula, in addition to Asiatic and African possessions. Under the vigorous leadership of their Grand Vizirs, the family of Kiuprili, the Turks aimed to consolidate their hold on Hungary, destroy the Hapsburg power in Eastern Europe, hold back the Poles from expanding toward the Black Sea, and check the Russian advance southward.

The Smaller States, the Swiss cantons (independent after 1648), supplying mercenaries to many kings, commanding important routes of communication, but playing no significant, independent rôle; the Netherlands, among the richest of European states, defending their thriving colonies and trade against English competition, and defending their very existence as a political entity against the expansion of France.

The Papacy and the Italian States, of less political significance than formerly; Venice, declining commercially, but still struggling against the Turks; Naples and Sicily (the two Sicilies), Tuscany, Parma, Piacenza, Milan, Genoa, and Savoy, mostly under the influence of one or the other of the greater states, as Spain, France, or the Hapsburgs. Papal influence was scarcely to be estimated as more than that of the other Italian states.

Taken as a whole, we may say that most of these European states fall into two groups according to the type of policy pursued by their governments. One group comprised the states which were struggling to defend their territories and independence; their policy might be described as passive, non-aggressive, and self-contained. The other group comprised the states aggressively endeavoring to expand their possessions and power. Generally speaking, Spain, most of the German states, Poland, Sweden, the Netherlands, and most of the Italian states were on the defensive, trying to maintain the status quo. France, Russia, the Turks, and among the German states, Brandenburg-Prussia, especially, were ambitiously on the offensive, aiming to expand territorially, and seeking more prestige and power. The Hapsburgs were, in a sense, in both groups; i.e., they were forced to be on the defensive by the nature of their dominions, their location, and the enterprise of their neighbors; at the same time, the Hapsburgs were ambitious, grasping, and aggressive. Their whole history is a maze of contradictions and inconsistencies, and it is not surprising to find them, paradoxically enough, in both groups of states. England hardly belongs in either category. She had no aggressive continental designs, and stood, on the continent, more or less on the defensive. She was concerned in the maintenance of the balance of power, and desired to see no state acquire a hegemony, nor did she intend to allow any strong state to lodge on the shore of the Low Countries. Economically, however, and in the colonial world, England was just beginning to take the initiative in acquisition. In these fields she was about to become decidedly aggressive.

What constitutes the explanation of such a difference between these seventeenth-century states? Why should the policy of one group be defensive, and of the other aggressive? Certainly, we may assume that as far as being eager for the glory and spoils of military victory is concerned, one state would be as prepared as any other to gain as much as possible. Limitations of size and resources, the weakness of their governments, and the proximity of strong neighbors, compelled many of them to remain on the defensive. What led the others to an aggressive policy? In other words, why were the larger and more powerful states constantly at war, or ready to fight? We must remember that most of the European states of the seventeenth century were controlled by dynasties, nearly absolute in power, and fortified by what they believed to be Divine Right. These dynasties could therefore conduct the policy of states as they saw fit. No consultation with their subjects was necessary, although it was true, of course, that important interests such as industry and commerce could at least present their desires to the sovereigns.

What was it that these dynastic kings pursued in their policies of state? For what purpose did they assume that God allowed them to reign over their respective states? Obviously, the answer given by any of them might have been: to protect their lands and peoples, to maintain law and order, to dispense justice, and to provide for the general welfare of their subjects. Such duties, we should say, as belonged to any government. Our search, however, is directed to the discovery of what these kings considered to be this *general welfare*. In this crucial question we find a most important bearing upon the whole history of royal dynasties, as well as of modern states. Seventeenth-century dynasties by Divine Right were commonly given to confusing the welfare of states and peoples with their own personal and family interests and ambitions, regarding them, in fact, as identical. What was good for the dynasty was good for the state.

The protection of lands and peoples, or security of the state as we now call it, was the chief professed concern of every government in the conduct of its relations with other states. Then, as now, ideas of security covered a multitude of possible interpretations. Instances are comparatively rare, since the sixteenth century, of wanton, unprovoked attack by one state upon another, and yet there have been innumerable wars, always declared by both sides to be wars of defence, of security. The explanation of this lies in the numerous possibilities in the interpretation of the meaning of what is necessary for security. The principle of security has generally been built on notions that the best defence is preparedness to fight. Such preparedness has frequently been carried to the extent of developing the theory that to attack first is necessary; an offensive will catch an enemy before he can attack, and thereby provide defence against him. Finally, security consists in the conviction that certain territories lying perhaps just over the borders of a state are indispensable for adequate defence,—they are strategically valuable for military operations in defence, or they constitute a natural barrier. Such considerations, it may easily be seen, can be applied to justify almost any policy, from a glaringly aggressive undertaking to a bona fide striving for security.

This has been true from the first modern war to the latest international conflict. How slowly men come to face realities, and judge events with reason and not with prejudices and emotions! It is very easy to see how, when decisions rested almost entirely with the head of a royal dynasty, whose regard for the state was that of an owner for his property and rights, matters of security might be subject to the temper and impatience of a hasty, overzealous and unrestrained individual. Conceptions of right and defence of right, particularly where land and wealth were concerned, might be, and frequently were, used to cover ambition and aggressiveness. No restraints existed, except limitations of strength and fear of more powerful rivals, to curb dynasties in their interpretation of security.

Power was undoubtedly the principal ambition of dynasties,—power and what it implies in exalted position, enviable influence, and the consciousness of controlling men and resources. How could power be obtained? In attempting to answer this question, we are dealing with a problem which has confronted man from the day when he first began to fight, to the present moment. The acquisition of territories and peoples seemed the obvious way to acquire power. Since organized society began, probably, kings, or their equivalents, have fought with one another for the possession of lands and peoples. It is only in very recent years that men have analysed this aim, and asked the question: Does the gaining of territories and peoples really mean the gaining of power? Such gains may satisfy the craving of an individual for authority, prestige, and the appearance of power; but in reckoning up the costs, and in attempting to estimate the effect of gains made by force upon the people involved, doubts have been cast upon the simple notion that vast territories, or numerous subjects, necessarily make for power,—or for the welfare of the state.

Mercantilist ideas undoubtedly convinced seventeenth-century monarchs of the validity of these conceptions of power. They hold that more land and more people implied more resources, more labor, therefore more trade and consequently more precious metal; hence the state would be more powerful. A policy for power was clearly one of the characteristics of seventeenth-century absolute monarchy.

Man's very ancient tradition of what constitutes human greatness, namely triumph by physical might, glory in martial victory—a special survival of feudal and chivalric sense of honor and glory—and the imposition, by force, of one will on another, must also be reckoned as another potent consideration of the kings as to what constituted the welfare of the state. Proud of their achievement in state making, dynastic monarchs could feel the vigor of their new strength, and, as ambitious, overbearing, and quarrelsome individuals, could use this strength in seeking what glory they would. Traditional association of kings, as in origin, the war leaders of their peoples, with ancient deeds of ancestors, and with the primitive hunter's instinct of striking to draw blood, combined to inspire kings to seek glory in arms. Their nobles, affected by similar traditions and instincts, readily followed. Their people also followed —and paid.

Guided by such considerations, policies of state were framed during the seventeenth century. The monarchs of the strong states could act with positive vigor, interpreting the welfare of their dominions in an aggressive fashion. Weaker states must be content with a more passive, defensive policy. France, as we have observed, was incontestably the most powerful of European states, and her monarch keenly sensitive of his preeminence. To Louis XIV, power, glory, and triumphs in arms were a consuming passion. At times his judgment and policy were subordinated to these influences. He was not, however, always so foolish as to abandon a sense of what was fundamentally for the welfare of France. Yet, at other times, the glory of the Bourbon dynasty led him, as in the case of the Spanish succession, into a war in which his dynasty would, in all probability, be much more benefited than his people. As a whole, the foreign policy of Louis XIV developed through two important phases. The first was concerned with the security of France; and the second was the aggrandizement of Dynastic Power. The first covered the period from 1661 to 1697, and entailed three great wars. The second covered the period from 1702 to 1713, and was devoted to a great war for making a Bourbon the lord of the Spanish inheritance.

The security of France Louis interpreted in the unrestrained, aggressive manner we have mentioned. To be safe, France must have her "natural frontiers," giving her the Rhine, the Alps, and the Pyrenees for boundaries. To be safe, she must have what was "rightfully" hers, namely the territories included in the ancient Roman province of Gaul. To be safe, she must have the strategic features just outside of her frontiers of 1660, namely the Rhine and the Alps. Thus we find Louis justifying his first three wars; the first (1664-1668), against Spain, to acquire the Spanish Netherlands as far as the Rhine and its mouths; netting him, at the Peace of Aix-la-Chapelle, a slice of territory extending France northwards; the second (1672-1678), against the Dutch, to complete the gains of the first war, and secure a firm strategic hold on the lower Rhine; netting him at the Peace of Nimwegen, more territory to the northwards, and, toward the Alps, the Franche-Comté; the third war (1688-1697), at first against Spain and some of the German states, to gain the Upper Rhine (Alsace and Lorraine), and ultimately against most of Europe which became alarmed at the extension of his power; netting him at the Peace of Ryswick, Strassburg and some of Alsace.

These wars were preceded and accompanied by a prodigious amount of subtle diplomatic maneuvering, by which Louis aimed to isolate his proposed victims, i.e., provide that friendly states which might possibly render assistance, should be bought off, or allied to France in such wise that they would not interfere. In all this, he was aided by the aggression of the Turks which distracted the attention of the Hapsburgs, and that of the Poles also; he was aided, furthermore, by the growing and expanding power of Russia which alarmed the Scandinavian states, Poland, and Branden-burg-Prussia; and especially was he favored by the internal troubles in England which weakened the strength of the Stuarts and actually made them, for a time, dependent on money supplied by Louis himself. As the successes of Louis' diplomacy and arms increased, the other European states became disturbed, fearing that he would not stop at the "natural frontiers" of France. They began to dread that the balance of power would be upset. Small states feared that they would be conquered and added to France; large states were concerned lest some of their lands be stripped away, and that the overweening power of Louis would subordinate them to the status of vassal or dependent states. The consequence was that many of these states began to make combinations against Louis; these alliances became stronger, and eventually wore down Louis' strength, and brought him to a halt. With so many enemies against him, he could make no further gains. Diplomacy and diplomatic combinations provided the means for preserving the balance of power, and perhaps prevented Louis XIV from anticipating the Napoleonic empire.

Hardly were these wars over, when diplomacy became much agitated over the ultimate fate of the vast Spanish dominions. Charles II of Spain was moribund, and had no direct heirs. If the whole succession (inheritance) went to any one of the already powerful dynasties, especially the Bourbon or Hapsburg, the balance of power would be seriously deranged, and Europe threatened with the dominion of a single dynasty. A series of complicated negotiations ensued, in which all the great states participated and arranged for a partition of Charles' empire as soon as he should die. Several states would share in the partition, no one gaining enough to become overwhelmingly strong. At the point of death, however, Charles II, angered at the presumption of the states in dismembering his empire, and inspired by a desire to leave the whole intact, made a will leaving the entire succession to Philip of Bourbon, grandson of Louis XIV. In spite of the provision in the will that the French and Spanish crowns should not be united, Europe regarded the arrangement of the will as a menace. There was no assurance that a series of deaths might not, after all, lead to the combination of the two crowns.

Realizing full well the opposition of Europe, Louis XIV nevertheless decided to support his grandson in accepting the inheritance. The greatness and glory of the House of Bourbon were involved. Louis himself could see his prestige and power extended through a member of his dynasty ruling in Spain. To accept the succession presumably meant war, but Louis accepted it. No great good, even in success, could accrue to France and her people. At best, Frenchmen could take pride in saying that a Frenchman ruled in Spain, but the French people must pay. The war came, and a great European combination fought to preserve the balance of power against the ambitions of the Bourbon dynasty. France bled and suffered for the pride of her king. We may find in the losses and wastage the basic causes of the great Revolution to come less than a century later.

In the end, Louis gained little but the empty satisfaction of seeing his grandson, Philip V, king of Spain. It is true that Spain was subsequently much under French influence, but the resources of Spain were so depleted that this was not of great assistance to France. The Spanish succession did not come to France; the balance of power was maintained. Besides the cost of the war, France lost valuable colonial opportunities to England. These later proved to be for England stepping stones for imperial successes against France. In the Treaty of Utrecht, England acquired from Spain Gibraltar and Minorca and an entrance to Spain's colonial trade (the Asiento). From Louis XIV she gained Nova Scotia, Newfoundland and the Hudson's Bay region, ominous signs of what was later to happen to the promising beginnings of a French empire in the heart of North America.

Thus ended, in war and diplomacy, the Age of Louis XIV. France had been led by her Sun King to a pinnacle of power and glory. Everywhere her influence in diplomacy and arms had been felt, and her example copied. French ideas and French policies were universally adopted, respected, and feared. Finally, however, came a check to all this greatness. Louis XIV had attempted too much. Ambition and dynastic pride led to excessive drain upon the strength of the state, and made possible the beginning of a progressive decline which ultimately worked into revolution. From the point of view of the place of France in the broader aspects of world influence, this decline was particularly tragic, because at this very time the possibilities of expansion into permanent world-wide importance were dawning.

FRENCH INFLUENCE BEYOND EUROPE

During the reign of Louis XIV, continents beyond Europe began to assume a new importance in the expansion of civilization. While to Louis and to those monarchs who imitated him, diplomacy and war seemed the most becoming business of kings; while Europe was dazzled by the glitter of Versailles, and by feats of arms, obscure men and women were daringly and painfully carrying the elements of civilization into regions much vaster than Europe. Interests other than those of dynastic monarchies and their continental ambitions were leading to the settlement of regions destined to change the nature of the European balance of power, and Old-World ideas. Religious and political dissatisfaction with home conditions led thousands of Europeans to seek new homes abroad; the expansion of commerce, and hopes of gain led thousands to explore new lands, seeking not merely treasure, but substantial opportunities for livelihood and trade. The race was to be not to the soldiers, but to the settlers.

The seventeenth century witnessed, in fact, a profound change from the European attitude which had been produced by the first century of discoveries and explorations. Then, gold and silver and new routes of navigation had impelled adventure; now, the forces underlying trade and colonization were operating. There came to Europe a more serious realization of the importance of possessing or controlling the imperial dominions beyond the seas. With the decline in the strength of Spain, Portugal, and Holland a freer field was left for other powers, notably for England and France. Rivalry between these ancient enemies for the control of the new opportunities was indeed inevitable. A second Hundred Years' War was bound to come.*

For such a contest France easily had the lead. Her size and resources, her more numerous population, the power and prestige of her government, all combined to furnish her with the most favorable advantages. France might well have become the first modern world

* Cf. A. H. Buffinton's *The Second Hundred Years War.* (Berkshire Studies, Holt.)

power, with an empire spreading into all the continents. Established by Cartier and Champlain in Canada, controlling important routes into the interior of America; established by Richelieu in the West Indies, in Africa, and in the Far East, France had initial opportunities certainly equal to those of her rival. Colbert saw these, and endeavored to develop them for the greatness and glory of Louis XIV. Besides his efforts to encourage commerce and industry, Colbert refounded the French colonial empire. The government and colonists of Canada were strengthened, becoming the Royal Province of New France. Trading companies were refurbished, or created, for the trade of the Baltic and the Levant, for Africa and the West Indies, and also for the East Indies.

Contemporaneously occurred a dramatic and stirring extension of French activity into yet new fields. A small group of intrepid Frenchmen explored and potentially brought under the influence of France as grand an empire as was ever offered a sovereign. This was the heart of the North American continent, with its marvellous network of waterways, the Ohio, Missouri, the Mississippi rivers, and the Great Lakes. Jesuits and fur traders, after incredible daring and fortitude, blazed the trail from the mouth of the St. Lawrence to the mouth of the Mississippi. Joliet (1645-1700) discovered the Niagara river, its falls and gorge, explored the way to Mackinac, Lake Winnebago, and the Wisconsin river. Supported by the energy of Frontenac, La Salle, Tonty, and Hennepin established French claims (1679) to the valley of the Ohio, and the land up to the

Alleghenies, thus hemming in the English colonies to a narrow strip of coastal territory. In 1682, La Salle crowned his adventures with another exploit. From the Great Lakes, by way of the Illinois, he reached the Mississippi, descended the river to the Gulf of Mexico, took possession of this "imperial" valley in the name of France, and christened it after the Sun King, Louisiana.

Thus was the way prepared for the expansion of France. With a language already becoming almost universal, a centralized and powerful government, a highly developed culture, and a recognized leadership in the fields of art and literature, an energetic and thriving population, France possessed the fairest prospects for extending and multiplying her influence. Something of all this she did accomplish. Few places once entered by French influence were left untouched by these contacts, but, in general, the glories of Louis XIV were limited to Europe. The vision was absent. Immediate, traditional, Old-World appeals were strongest, and the future was lost. The wars and diplomacy which we have noted absorbed French strength. Louvois had triumphed over Colbert, and under the star of England, the course of empire took its way.

THE PRINCIPAL TREATIES OF THE REIGN OF LOUIS XIV
SHOWING THE CHIEF FRENCH GAINS

1659—*Peace of the Pyrenees.* France and Spain.
> France acquires: Roussillon, Conflans, Cerdagne and towns in Artois, Flanders, Hainault, and Lorraine.

Louis XIV to marry Maria Theresa, eldest daughter of Philip IV, of Spain.

1668—*Peace of Aix-la-Chapelle*. France and Spain. (War of Devolution.)

France acquires: Towns on fringe of Spanish Netherlands such as Lille, Tournai, Oudenarde.

1678-1679—*Peace of Nimwegen*. France, Holland, Spain, Sweden, Denmark, and the Emperor. (The "Dutch War.")

France acquires: Franche-Comté, and several towns on the fringe of the Spanish Netherlands, as Valenciennes, Ypres, Cambray, St. Omer, Maubeuge, and Condé.

1697—*Peace of Ryswick*. France, England, Spain, the Empire, and Holland. (War of the League of Augsburg.)

France acquires: Strassburg, and claims in Alsace.

1698—*First Treaty of Partition*. (Never operative.) Dividing the Spanish Empire.

France to have: Naples, Sicily, and ports in Tuscany.

Bavaria to have: Spain, the Indies, and the Spanish Netherlands.

Austria to have: Milan.

1700—*Second Treaty of Partition*. (Never operative.)

France to have: Naples, Sicily, Lorraine.

Austria to have: Spain and the Indies.

Lorraine to have: Milan.

1713—*Peace of Utrecht*. France, England, Holland, Savoy, Prussia, Spain, Portugal.

France cedes to England: Newfoundland, Nova Scotia, Hudson Bay.

France destroys fortifications of Dunkirk.

France places a Bourbon, Philip V, grandson of Louis XIV, on the throne of Spain.

CHAPTER III

THE INTELLECTUAL ACHIEVEMENTS OF
THE "GREAT AGE"

NOT so very long ago it was possible to satisfy the
ordinary demands made upon the "history of an age"
by recounting the story of its wars, the changes of its
governmental forms, and the succession of its kings.
We have now come to realize, however, that our understanding of the past is inadequate without some knowledge of those other forms of human activity which have
been built into the foundations of the present. Civilization as it exists is quite as much the product of the
thought, of the literary and artistic expression, and of
the scientific conceptions of preceding centuries as it is
of their wars and political experiences. All that we are
is the consequence of all that our predecessors have
been and thought. Completely to revive the past, in
all its detail, to describe the life of the peasant as well
as that of the king, to record the totality of everyday
life as well as that of critical or dramatic episodes,
might well be the aim of the historian. Such, however,
is an ideal more easily stated than attained.

So numerous and ramified, so varied and elusive are
the many factors which comprise even the intellectual
aspect of a civilization, that it is well-nigh impossible
to present them all at once, even though we do not
confuse the picture by bringing in also the political,

social, and economic features. It is undeniably true that all these elements—intellectual, political, social, economic, religious, and others—constitute what is called the unity of history. Each is a vital part of the life of the human race. No one is necessarily more important than any other. To discriminate, on the basis of importance, is often necessary, but also often unfair or prejudiced. To omit any one of them tends to destroy the unity. For this reason, we sometimes confine our attention to a limited portion of the past and examine, as we are here trying to do, as many features as possible of one of the many "ages" of history. Yet even within a single age, we are confronted with this complexity, this baffling multiplicity of things. If, therefore, we try to see them all, we are subject to hopeless confusion; we cannot see the forest for the trees. In addition to this multiplicity, we have also to encounter the fact that each of the many elements concerned is in the process of change. No one is fixed and definite. Each is the result of preceding changes, some of which must be understood to explain its existence at a given moment. All are not, moreover, in similar stages of change at the same time; nor are they changing at the same rate.

To avoid some of these embarrassing difficulties, we try to generalize, i.e., we try to determine certain outstanding characteristics of the manifold features comprising the life of a period, to select what is common to many, and then to group all of them together. Thus we try to find a keynote or generalization which will explain a whole period. Such is, of course, only a rough and ready method. Many aspects must be omitted, many exceptions ignored, and an unwarranted emphasis must sometimes be placed. With these limitations in mind, we may approach a survey of the intellectual achievements of the Age of Louis XIV. To include every phase of intellectual activity between 1650 and 1700 will be manifestly impossible; merely to mention the individuals busy in intellectual fields would mean little more than giving a long list of names and dates. We must therefore select, and employ limited generalization, bearing in mind that what we here present is selected, and based, in part, upon generalization. Our study is not comprehensive or exhaustive.

LITERATURE

It has been commonly stated that literature in France during the Age of Louis XIV was subjected to the "reign of order and authority." The magnificent assertion of royal power by the king, and the glories of Versailles, imposed upon the minds of Frenchmen and other Europeans a sense of authority. Accustomed to look to Louis for political guidance, for the fashions in etiquette, deportment, and taste, men came to look to him for inspiration in ideas, and for the form of their expression. He in no wise disappointed such expectations. His conception of the rôle of an absolute monarch quite as easily accommodated the thought of himself as the source of ideas and taste as of law and government. Order, obedience, and regularity were his ideals for the political realm, and they dominated his notions of excellence in literature and in art.

As Louvois and Colbert were commissioned to regularize and control the affairs of the army, the finances, and industry, so the king believed that His Majesty could centralize and direct the literary and artistic expressions of his subjects. So great, indeed, was the prestige of France that many peoples who were not his subjects were influenced to follow French leadership and inspiration. Colbert undertook to direct the writers, painters, architects, and sculptors of France as though he were directing officials in his departments of administration. Through membership in the Academies, created and sanctioned by royal authority, and through the patronage of pensions, he accomplished much toward producing uniformity and compliance with the royal ideas of excellence in art and letters.

In spite of such regimentation, however, the total contribution of France under Louis XIV to the world's literature was by no means restricted to that inspired by the king, or that produced through his influence. Much of the subject matter, it is true, dealt with themes befitting monarchy and so great a king. Much of the tone and color were affected by Versailles and its grandeur; much of the adulation and flattery grew out of the cult of majesty. Beyond all these, there developed qualities which make the work of Louis' period the most thoroughly representative of all French literature, and distinctly characteristic of what is called French genius.

Throughout Europe, during the seventeenth century, the influence of the Renaissance upon literature was still strong. This influence consisted not only of an interest in the literature of Greece and Rome, but also in an attempt to apply the qualities manifested in Greek and Roman writing. These qualities are to be found in the subject matter of ancient poems, prose, and drama, and more especially in the form and manner of expression; they are also to be found in the thought or philosophy which were the sources of their inspiration. A sense of proportion, moderation, and dignity were the ideals of expression; the deeper problems of life, the more serious emotions of man, such as love, ambition, jealousy, and hate constituted the "classical" subjects most deserving treatment. Such matters and such forms constituted what was known as the classical tradition; classical, not merely because inspired by the classics, i.e., Greek and Roman literature, but also because they constituted a recognized, standard form and manner.

To work splendidly with such materials, and in such a manner, the Age of Louis XIV was most appropriately fitted. The grandeur and majesty of the king provided a background and an inspiration. French ability, or genius, provided the tools. These tools, which are considered peculiarly characteristic of France, were method of thinking, logical sequence of ideas, and lucidity of style. Not long before the advent of Louis XIV, Montaigne (1533-1592) contributed, in his studies of human nature, a skillful and searching analysis of ideas, gracefully and delicately expressed. Descartes (1596-1650) produced a method of thinking, a sense of order and logical arrangement. Malherbe (1555-1628) taught the use of plain, clear, precise, and concise language. These men influenced not French writers alone, but also the thinkers and writers of all Europe. Their work assisted notably in the establishment of French leadership throughout the world of letters. Their French successors, thus inspired, took up the classical tradition and handled it with fine insight and proportion, with national originality, felicity and skill, "making one of the most famous and unparalleled combinations in the history of literature."

Of these successors, Corneille (1606-1684), Molière (1622-1673), and Racine (1639-1699) constituted a group of dramatists whose names are still a by-word. Corneille, called the father of the French theater, employed legendary and historical settings for the presentation of his ideas; he did not intend to create historical dramas, although he occasionally reproduced the spirit of an historical period. He used such titles as *The Cid*, from medieval Spain, *Medea*, from ancient Greek legend, *Pompey*, from Republican Rome, *Theodore*, from early Christianity, *Attila*, from the Barbarian invasions, and *Heraclius* from the Byzantine Empire. All are but the majestic setting for his portrayal of the qualities of men, and the motives of their actions, particularly their political motives. Roman characters are numerous in his works, for "Roman history is the most political of histories."

His plays reflected the monarchical background of the age, and picture, in the guise of classical trappings, the political maxims and life of the seventeenth century. His verse is eloquent and sonorous, revealing with skill and power, the conflict of will with passion. He was preeminently the poet of the human will, "revealing man struggling against the blows of Fate, and prevailing against them, by means of his trust in himself and in the inward strength with which he feels himself endowed." In subject matter, form, and treatment Corneille renewed admirably the classical tradition, invigorated it, made it French, and prolonged its influence through civilized Europe. As Faguet says, "Corneille remains the very type of those artists who aspire towards the things that are great and who hold that the highest kind of beauty is to be found in the beauty of holiness."

In Molière, the Age of Louis XIV contributed generously to the development of modern comedy. His works are a permanent treasure of civilization. Many of his characters, like those of Shakspere, display ideas and even gestures which have become proverbial; he has described the classic hypocrite, the social climber, the legal pedant, the pretentious physician, the absurd and over-refined intellectual. In depicting these types, Molière has shown "a depth of conception, which is a very different thing from mere close observation of life, and which consists in the creation of characters capable of being viewed from ever fresh standpoints, and possessing an inexhaustible interest for those who subject them to analysis so that they offer a new revelation to readers of each successive generation." Molière aimed to teach, to exercise moral control; he was an eloquent expounder of morality. He laughed at the smug, affected imitation of the social ambitions of his time, and stripped sham and pretense naked to the eyes of the world. Moreover, he helped to produce good taste and to inculcate good manners. He has been called, in fact, the law giver of good manners. In this he was indeed, a worthy subject of "le grand monarque."

With Racine, the classical tradition was carried, in tragedy, even beyond the work of Corneille. In elegance, formality, and polish, Racine exceeded his contemporary, and has been said to have surpassed even the Greeks in his appreciation of human passion, bringing "the sweet harmony of poetry and the grace of language" to a higher point than any of his predecessors. He studied primarily the passions of love, jealousy, and ambition, and painted them with subtlety and delicacy. Like Corneille, he placed his figures against ancient legendary, and historical backgrounds and many of his titles such as *Phèdre, Iphigénie, Andromaque, Mithridate,* and *Britannicus* maintained the classical atmosphere.

To the work of these men France owes, also, those remarkable qualities of her language which, as we have observed, were acquired during the seventeenth century. Through the supreme excellence of usage at the hands of such writers, French became definitely established as one of the best vehicles of expression developed by occidental civilization. Conscious of this possession, the royal authority, operating through Colbert, endeavored to fix the standard of the language. The Academy was created by Richelieu between 1634 and 1637, "to give certain words to our language and to render it pure." With a membership of forty men of distinction (the "forty immortals") it was to represent, in the realm of language and literature, that authority based upon tradition and reason which is the essence of classicism. It was entrusted with the compilation of a great dictionary of the French language, as well as the production of a grammar. The custody of this task is still one of the functions of the Academy; but it was so slow in the early stages of the task that individual scholars, like Furetière and Richlelet brought out dictionaries before the end of the seventeenth century.

More effective, however, than the authority of dictionary or grammar in the definite fixing of the language was the development of a prose usage. Many writers naturally, of every sort, contributed to this, but none more so than Pascal (1623-1662). In his *Lettres Provinciales,* published in 1657, just before Louis XIV assumed the reins of government, he produced what has been called the first work of genius in modern French prose. He united in these letters all forms of eloquent expression; very few of the words which he used have undergone, to this day, any significant changes of meaning. Pascal was also important in the intellectual contributions of this period because, as a mathematician and physicist, he applied the scientific method of thinking, developed by Descartes, to religious problems.

A religious ferment was active in the seventeenth century, growing out of the vigorous spiritual zeal of the followers of Jansen (Jansenius, a Flemish bishop, 1585-1638). The Jansenists held that true religion depended upon the spiritual communion of man with God and, somewhat after the manner of St. Augustine and Calvin, they believed that salvation came by the grace of God. Inclined toward mysticism, and urging reform of the worldly and unspiritual aspects of the Church, they regarded, as spiritually inadequate, the ordinary manifestations of religion, i.e., going to church, participating in worship, and other forms of Christian duty. This brought the Jesuits into the field as defenders of the orthodox or conventional religious beliefs and practices. Worldly, politically minded, and power-seeking, the Jesuits succeeded in procuring a papal condemnation of the Jansenists as heretics. In the course of the struggle, however, the Jansenists at their French headquarters, Port Royal, an abbey on the outskirts of Paris, had gathered a number of learned and literary theologians. Pascal joined conflict with the Jesuits in defence of Port Royal and the Jansenists.

His "Provincial Letters" ventured an assault on dogmatic authority, and with unmatched satire he dared to meet the theologians on their own ground. He "voiced a new spirit" in the discussions of religious affairs, and gave a strong impetus to the free handling of matters which had hitherto been a closed preserve for ecclesiastical authorities. Port Royal was ultimately suppressed, but the cause of the Jansenists lived on, to become an active feature in the quarrels between Crown and Parlement, which helped to precipitate the Revolution of 1789.

Pascal's freedom was not the only challenge to authority and orthodoxy, even in the monarchy of a Louis XIV. All initiative and variety in thought and expression were not stifled by the dictatorship of Versailles. In the *Critical Dictionary* of Pierre Bayle (1647-1706), a Calvinist who was banished to Rotterdam, appeared a form of criticism generally regarded as a forerunner of the work of Voltaire. Inspired by an eager, historical curiosity, Bayle sought the explanation of how and why things came to be what they were, and naturally found that many of the accepted ideas were based on errors or absurd prejudices. He was keen, ironical, and not very reverent in exposing misconceptions. Not only Voltaire, in his style and purposes, but also Diderot and the other Encyclopedists owed much to the example and inspiration of Bayle.

Another somewhat similar and stimulating influence arising during this age, and destined to extend to other times and places, was the intellectual turmoil produced by the "quarrel between the Ancients and the Moderns." Of the importance of the classical tradition we have already spoken; the thought, manner, and substance of ancient literature were appropriately the accepted cultural standard of the Europe of Louis XIV. Antiquity was regarded as the golden age of man's intellectual power and creativeness. The present and future could not hope to do much more than imitate. Against this conventional belief, however, protests had occasionally arisen, and by a sort of historical irony, the first real outburst of objection occurred in the very heart of Louis' reign.

In 1687, at a meeting of the French Academy, Charles Perrault read a poem entitled "The Century of Louis the Great," in which he maintained that the Ancients were not so wonderful, that they were not to be so slavishly worshipped, and that the men of the Age of Louis XIV, the Moderns, were equally great, if not actually greater. This was a bombshell. The very idea of setting Molière, for example, above Aristophanes, or Descartes above Plato, was blasphemy. A hubbub immediately arose. Boileau (1636-1711), a poet, satirist, and critic who was much admired, undertook the defence of the Ancients and the classical tradition. Defending the Moderns and, one may say, the present and the future, was Fontenelle (1657-1757), a nephew of Corneille, and a man of varied intellectual interests. With a fund of common sense, and an ability to clarify abstruse and technical matters, he championed the critical point of view. In his ingenious *Dialogues of the Dead,* he had even anticipated Perrault's attack on the Ancients. The *Quarrel* developed, and other adherents joined either side; it continued indefinitely, even to the present; it roused echoes in England and elsewhere. Its significance is primarily to be found in the contribution which it made to a new outlook on history and life. The past came to be regarded, not as something inherently more glorious and better than the present, but rather as the source of the present. A new optimism eventually grew out of this view, regarding the present as good, and even better than the past. Thus, the conception of progress was born; man began, rightly or wrongly, during the eighteenth and nineteenth centuries to believe that continued improvement, or progress, was possible. With this conception, the scientific theories of evolution, and the political theories of democracy, and social theories of "uplift," have naturally become closely associated.

To the many literary achievements thus wrought in the reign of Louis XIV, must be added others too numerous to be observed in detail. In richness and variety they are scarcely excelled by the work of any other period. Supplementing the influence of Molière in the development of taste, were the *Maxims* of the Duke of La Rochefoucauld (1613-1680). Short and pithy, these maxims were widely read; in a vivid and yet delicate manner they exposed the weakness and frailties of human nature, cynically attributing to self-interest, most human motives. The king frowned upon La Rochefoucauld although his sharp tongue lashed mankind in general, rather than the régime of Louis in particular. In the poetry of La Fontaine (1621-1695), grace and simplicity combine with an orginality and ingenuity which entitle the author to a place among the great writers of his age. The "most poetical of the French poets," La Fontaine exhibited a joy of living, a universal sympathy, and a spontaneity which enlivened his celebrated *Contes* (Fables) and made them a living picture of human life, and French society. He was not a naturalist, but in his stories he employed animals with marvellous skill for the delineation of human character. His vivacious and picturesque treatment of animal traits excel the solemn work of Æsop and other writers from whom he borrowed liberally.

The *Memoirs* of Cardinal de Retz (1614-1679) were another important contribution to the growth of the French language, and also to the field of literary effort. Active in the politics of the hectic days preceding the accession of Louis XIV, De Retz knew the world and its leaders; in his writings he has left penetrating and clear-cut portraits of notable figures: Richelieu, Mazarin, La Rochefoucauld, and others. As an historian he was not accurate or truthful, but in his psychological analysis of men he was extraordinarily proficient. His *Memoirs* are significant as writing of the highest class, and also for the fact that he placed this form of historical record on a plane with the other surpassing literature of the age. Somewhat similarly, Madame de Sévigné (1626-1696) maintained for the art of letter-writing a recognized place in an age of great literature. Simple and conversational, excellent in style, her letters reflect intimately and faithfully the aristocratic life of the seventeenth century, especially the salons, their personalities and their ideas. De Retz and Madame de Sévigné are only outstanding figures among a host of other writers of memoirs and letters who enriched the literature of this age.

Formal eloquence was most profusely contributed, during this century, in the sermons and funeral orations of Bossuet (1627-1704) and Bordaloue (1632-1704). In lofty sentiments, fine words, and emotional appeal, these preachers dominated the imaginations of their contemporaries. Bossuet applied his oratorical powers to the recounting of history. In his *Discourse on Universal History,* composed for the instruction of the dauphin, he described the majestic power of government, the rise and fall of empires, and the manifestations of God's will among mankind. Bossuet reasserted the importance of the theological interpretation of history and emphasized the necessity of viewing history as a whole. Like the dramatists, these preachers exerted a considerable influence upon the development of spoken French.

Not strictly to be classed among the creators of literature, but none the less important among the literary figures of this age, were a group of learned Frenchmen whose energy and power vastly increased the amount of literary knowledge and the means of dealing with it. Among many other men of erudition, or savants, Casaubon (1559-1614), Scaliger (1540-1609), Ducange (1610-1688), and Mabillon (1632-1707) have rarely, if ever, been excelled. Mastering the vocabularies and structures of ancient languages, compiling dictionaries, studying manuscripts, coins, and inscriptions, they virtually created the tools with which the modern world has worked in acquiring its knowledge of the past. They introduced the means for a scientific study of language (philology), of historical manuscripts (diplomatics), of inscriptions (epigraphy), of coins (numismatics); their labors laid the foundations for what we call scholarship in the study of ancient and medieval civilizations by making available their records and the means of working with them. A number of these men were associated with the Benedictine Community of St. Maur, where, reviving some of the best monastic traditions of the Middle Ages, the monks undertook vast collaborative works in the study of history. The accumulation of knowledge has subsequently led modern students in many fields to follow this example of collaboration.

Outside of France, the chief literary productions of the Age of Louis XIV were those of England. Shakspere had died at the beginning of the century (1616), and the decades that followed saw no great group of men comparable to the Elizabethans, or to the Frenchmen of this century. John Milton (1608-1674) was almost solitary in his splendor. Although he was the high champion of the Calvinist régime in the commonwealth, he was none the less, like his French contemporaries, imbued with the classical tradition. His *Paradise Lost* is not only religious in theme, it is also classical in its mythology, in its form, and in its sonorous magnificence. Bunyan (1628-1688), in his *Pilgrim's Progress,* also reflecting the Puritan interest of the times, created the greatest of Christian allegories. Dryden (1631-1700), poet and dramatist, developed a poetic satire of some strength, though of no great nobility.

Aside from these men, English literature was not, during this period, prolific in great works. The political controversies raised by the conflict of king and Parliament, however, stimulated much thought upon government and its problems; and resulted in several writings of importance. Thomas Hobbes (1588-1679), a philosopher, wrote the *Leviathan,* undertaking to explain the relationship between man and society, between the individual and government. He conceived of the State as an organism made up of the individuals who live within it—a huge being like the Leviathan of Scripture. The power which controls the State is supreme and irresponsible, vested in the monarch and theoretically exercised for the welfare of all. In his analysis of this power, Hobbes influenced later thought and writing on politics by his rational method and his historical judgment. John Locke (1632-1704), also a philosopher, influenced by the work of Descartes, sought even more than Hobbes to apply reasonableness to the problems of politics. In his *Letters on Toleration* and *Treatises on Government,* he tried to find a rational basis for civil liberty. In justifying the Glorious Revolution of 1688, he developed the so-called *contract theory* of government, in which he held that people and their rulers agree respectively to obey and govern for the welfare of all. When kings govern badly, they have broken their part of this contract, and the people are justified in revolting; they are obligated to remove the king. Rousseau and the American Revolutionary leaders were profoundly influenced by these ideas of Locke.

In other countries, comparatively little of general literary significance was produced. In the Netherlands, the Portuguese Jew, Spinoza (1632-1677), developed from the philosophic ideas of Descartes a new conception of God and nature, midway between the Revelation of dogmatic theology, and the skepticism of the agnostics. In Germany, Leibnitz (1646-1716), with amazing versatility, made important contributions in philosophy, mathematics, and literature. His scientific influence we shall note below. In Spain, French influence was possibly less than anywhere else. Spanish writers pursued their own way, indifferent to the currents of other places. Some of their forms and tastes, indeed, were borrowed by their French neighbors; but with the death of Lope de Vega in 1635, their most original creative genius passed away.

No one people, as we have stated, and few other periods, have been so prolific in literary production and general influence as the French of the seventeenth century. Rarely has a single period made so many and such permanent contributions. In the drama, in the portrayal of manners and modes through memoirs and letters, in formal eloquence, in scientific and religious prose, in the perfection of language, and in the tools with which it is studied, the period of Louis XIV was indeed a "Great Age."

ART

Architecture

An age is sometimes more faithfully reflected in its buildings than in any of its more conscious records. Architecture is the result of a definite demand; it meets practical needs, and it satisfies existing requirements in taste. From its forms, therefore, we may judge what a period wanted for its own uses, and what it thought to be attractive and beautiful. Other pictures of an age, such as we find in literature, are often more conscious, i.e., they are subject to the originality and personality of the author who is making them. Prejudices, preferences, and purposes may creep, more easily, into a written record. Less significantly do they appear in stone, brick, or wooden structures. A Gothic church, for example, is quite as complete, as honest, and as unprejudiced an account of medieval thought, needs, and taste as could be imagined. The revival of classic forms and ideals by the Renaissance builders revealed clearly a renewed interest in Greek and Roman buildings. In this, the Italians were the leaders, and, for a long time, were the teachers of Europe.

By the seventeenth century, however, Italian influence was beginning to wane. The people of the new European states were seeking to meet their architectural needs according to their own ideas. They still admired classical traditions; and the forms of Greek and Roman buildings inspired their construction; but there was a new, independent manner in the application of this inspiration. At the hands of the Italians, the classical forms of the Renaissance had, in the sixteenth century, been modified into what is called the baroque style of architecture. (Baroque, from the Portuguese, baroco, meaning irregularly shaped pearl.) This style presents a straining for colossal effects, disregarding classical proportion and regularity. Huge, almost grotesque ornamentation, curved and twisted lines, characterized the baroque. Interiors, particularly those of churches decorated in the baroque manner, were sometimes described as being decorated in the "Jesuit style," because they aimed to dazzle the eye by

the wealth and variety of motives, to captivate by striking effects. Competing with the popularity of the baroque, especially outside of Italy, was the "academic"
style which aimed, during the seventeenth century, to
reproduce more faithfully and accurately the proportions and simplicity of the classical architecture.

Under Louis XIV, French architects carried the academic style to predominance, and created a distinctly
French type of classical architecture. Versailles, as
we have seen, was an inspiration for much European
imitation. In addition to the construction of churches
and palaces, which had for centuries been the principal
forms of architectural expression, the France of the
Great Age witnessed the application of architectural
efforts to the construction of buildings for purposes
other than religion or princely habitation. The creation
of squares, or open spaces, in cities, as for example at
Paris or Nancy, surrounded by fine buildings to be
used as stores and residences, was undertaken. Notions for the appropriate planning for cities appeared.
Blocks of houses of improved and interesting design
were erected. Interiors were planned more in conso-
nance with the needs of comfortable, domestic living
than had been the case with palaces. Greater variety
in the use of building materials was attempted; combinations of brick and stone enlivened the hitherto
rather drab monotony of great structures. In Paris,
one of the finest sections of the vast Louvre was built
by the architects of Louis XIV, presenting what has
been described as the "finest view of a palace in existence"; the great Place Vendôme and the Place des

Victoires were erected, and two notable city gates, several churches, the astronomical observatory, the Institute of France, and the Invalides were among the architectural triumphs of the time.

In architecture, as in literature, the English were perhaps next to the French, the chief creative influence of the seventeenth century. In England, also, the academic or more purely classical manner prevailed over the baroque. Inigo Jones (1573-1652) designed the banqueting hall of Whitehall Palace, and influenced the design of the country houses which the great land owners were beginning to construct in this period. The great fire of 1666, at London, gave an unusual opportunity for the genius of Sir Christopher Wren (1632-1723). He designed the new St. Paul's Cathedral, erected the Fire Monument, a column inspired by Trajan's column at Rome, and planned many churches for London. The spires which he placed on these structures were particularly successful, and it is to be observed that their influence is still to be seen in the white steeple of many a New England colonial church. In England, too, the new form of group construction was applied in such instances as Covent Garden in London, and at Bath, the celebrated watering place in the west of England.

Germany, devastated by the Thirty Years' War, and economically much crippled, was the scene of comparatively little building in this century, and few architectural creations were undertaken.

Painting

More independence appeared in the painting of pictures than in any other form of seventeenth-century artistic expression. Less influenced by tradition, by the Italian past, or by French leadership, the painters of the Netherlands and Spain, especially, developed vigorous "national" schools, reflecting a variety of interests and original conceptions. In France, painting, like literature and architecture, was subjected to the authority and taste of the monarch. The Academies of Architecture and Painting, which had been founded to centralize and direct artistic effort, were accorded by Colbert a virtual monopoly of instruction in the arts, and in the control of patronage. In 1666, Colbert founded the French Academy in Rome, where scholarships were provided for six painters, four sculptors and two architects. He desired that French artists should learn all that the Italians had to teach, but he desired the development of a distinctly French manner. As in literature and architecture, the classic or academic forms were sought in painting. These are clearly evident in the work of two celebrated Frenchmen.

Poussin (1594-1665) and Gellée (1600-1682) were both greatly influenced by Italian paintings, and in their pictures, subjects from classical mythology, Italian landscapes, and academic restraint may be observed. Grandeur, so much evidenced by the court of the Sun King, and a cold, formal delicacy mark their work. In the pictures of Gellée, more commonly called from the region of his origin, Lorraine, there is, however, a radiance of skies, glory of clouds, and weirdness of light which influenced one of the greatest of modern painters—Turner. Some of the paintings of Lorraine and Turner, hanging side by side in the National Gallery in London, are an interesting example of the ties which exist even between remotely separated ages.

A group of court painters, Rigaud, Le Seur, Mignard, and Philippe de Champaigne recorded, in their portraits, the appearance of the leading men in the France of Louis XIV. None of this work, however, achieved the distinction attained by portrait painters in other lands. In gorgeous frescoes, covering the vast ceilings of Versailles and the new churches in Paris, celebrating the glories of Louis, we find their most characteristic work; but it was done in a conceited and much over-praised manner. It exerted comparatively little permanent influence beyond France. Toward the end of Louis' life, however, a new vigor came into French painting. Centering at Paris, removed from the stifling control of Versailles, younger men created a new school. Among these the leader was Watteau (1684-1721). With a light and delicate touch, he pictured the graceful, colorful, and romantic aspects of aristocratic life. Gay and fanciful, his pastoral scenes were a delightful contrast to the heavier, more grandiose court pictures of the academic school.

Spain, in the Age of Louis XIV, produced not only a native originality in painting, but also one of the world's greatest painters. Velasquez (1599-1660) was one of the supreme masters of technique, i.e., he possessed the ability to execute with surpassing skill the ideas which he conceived. His subjects ranged from the portrayal of religious and mythological scenes to pictures of everyday life, historic groups, and the portraits of the anæmic Hapsburg court of Madrid. In color, composition, and atmosphere his works are among the most celebrated. Murillo (1618-1682) painted devout and sentimental Virgins, and boys and girls of the streets. His rich and vaporous colors, his ethereal and yet realist treatments, and his tender and sensuous pity, have given his work a strong popular appeal, but it is, in general, commonplace when compared with the strong, deeper painting of Velasquez. In the paintings of Ribera (1588-1656) and of Zurburan (1598-1663) there is an interesting reflection of Spanish character and contemporary religious feeling. Ecstatic monks, religious fervor, the ravages of torture and martyrdom, starving beggars, and the wrinkles of old age are portrayed with a realism and ferocity which are both daring and impressive.

Most appealing, in many ways, is the seventeenth-century contribution in pictures made by the painters of the Netherlands. These pictures were distinctly different, in purpose and manner, from what pictures had been before. Hitherto, most paintings had been made for the decoration of churches or palaces, to adorn altars, or to please sovereigns or other munificent patrons. In the Protestant portion of the Netherlands, i.e., in Holland, churches were severely without decoration, and palaces were not numerous. There were, however, many merchants whose successful trade had provided them with the means for buying pictures.

Paintings of a relatively small size, therefore, suitable for private houses were desired. Large canvases, indeed, were executed for town halls and gild houses, portraying groups of town officials, the members of the many associations of communal life, officers of the militia, archery clubs, merchant gilds, and so on. It is for the small, household pictures, however,—delightful to live with,—that the Dutch are perhaps most to be admired. Subject matter varied notably from the religious scenes, mythological and courtly compositions of earlier painting. A new world is spread upon canvas; sketches of popular life in inns, or at village fêtes; domestic incidents; the activity of a quay; landscapes; animals; the labor of a farm; musicians and what not.

The Dutch masters of Delft, Haarlem, and Amsterdam developed remarkable technical skill; they did not aim to tell stories, to represent literature or history in painting. They did not attempt the glories of either heavenly or worldly powers. They reflected the life of Holland in the seventeenth century, and with marvellous ability, they set it forth in the atmosphere and color of its natural surroundings. Franz Hals (d. 1666) has been called the "laureate of laughter" from the skill with which he reproduced, in his unrivalled portraits, various manifestations of mirth. His individuals, singly and in the wonderful groups on his canvases, revealed the prosperous Dutch burghers, not kings, princes, saints or angels; they contained men and women of the middle classes, physicians, lawyers, farmers, musicians, and merchants. In the work of the "prodigious" Jan ver Meer of Delft (1637-1675) were some of the rarest qualities, which have in this twentieth century come to be particularly appreciated. One of the world's most celebrated landscapes, *A View of Delft,* came from his brush; his scenes of Dutch interiors, warm with sunlight, show not only a remarkable handling of light, but also reveal, in an intimate and fascinating way, the neatness and comfort of domestic life. Among other details of these Dutch homes, it is interesting to observe that many an interior reveals at least one wall decorated with a map. These maps reflect the far-flung commerce and maritime activities of seventeenth-century Holland. Pieter de Hoogh, Metzu, Dou, and Terborch, among numerous others, are also especially to be mentioned as brilliantly rendering bright and cozy middle-class homes, with perfect technique. Van Ruisdael and Hobbema, with landscapes, which are still widely popular, Wouwerman with horses and horsemen, Paul Potter and Cuyp with their incomparable animals were all masters of the first rank.

These men carried to the highest success what is called *genre* painting, i.e., pictures dealing realistically with scenes from everyday life, as distinguished from historic, heroic, romantic, or ideal themes. Jan Steen was one of the most interesting of these genre painters, with his jolly feasts, his peasant children with their animal pets, his happy family groups. At the hands of such men, it has been said, "art, that had so long been at the service only of the church and the proud, became suddenly, without losing any of its divinity, a fireside friend." Rembrandt (1606-1669) was, and probably still remains, the most celebrated of Dutch

painters. He has been called "the greatest painter
that the north of Europe has produced." Excelling in
portraits, magnificent with such groups as "The Night
Watch"—which is really not a night watch, at all, but a
group of arquebusiers leaving their Hall in broad day-
light,—subtle in his rendering of light and shade, he
presented an extraordinary range of subjects. Some
of his pictures touched religious themes, some were
genre paintings, but none were more indicative of his
age and the broadened scope of art than his "School of
Anatomy," which presents Doctor Tulp lecturing before a dissected body, to a group of surgeons.

In what is now the Belgian portion of the Netherlands, especially at Antwerp, flourished another school
of master painters—the Flemish. Peter Paul Rubens
(1577-1640) painted an unparalleled number of pictures, many of them enormous canvases. His conceptions were grandiose; mythological themes, battles of
gods, riotous Bacchanalian orgies; religious subjects
and historical scenes, such as the huge series in the
Louvre representing the apotheosis of Henry IV and
Marie de Medici. He was an eloquent narrator, theat-
rical, and florid, and an extremely rich colorist. His
work has been likened to the baroque or Jesuit style of
architecture, dazzling and seductive. Van Dyke (1599-
1631) was another of the Flemish painters. His most
notable work was portraiture. Living much in England, he was distinctly a court painter, executing, during his short life, hundreds of portraits of the royal
family and the aristocracy. These portraits are valuable historical documents, for they reveal the psychol-

ogy of important people more faithfully, perhaps, than could be done by any other medium. Among the Flemish genre painters was David Teniers (1610-1690). Inspired by Rubens, he became one of the greatest painters of peasants. His brilliant rendering of fairs, wine-shops, drinking bouts, and farmyard scenes have preserved the life and color of the seventeenth century in a most vivid manner.

Compared with the fresh and vigorous work of the Spaniards and the Dutch and the Flemish, painting in Italy, Germany, and England was not notable in this century. Sculpture was nowhere of the highest, creative order, although some works of permanent merit were executed in France. Statues and busts of Louis XIV were naturally in demand, and some excellent ones were produced. It was, however, only when the limitations of allegory, and the glorifications of the king were removed, that works of genius appeared. Puget (1622-1694), Coysevox (1640-1720), and his pupils, the Coustous, sculptured some glorious statues. The spirited "Horses of Marly," now at the entrance of the Champs Elysées, were perhaps the foremost work of the period.

Industrial Art

In architecture and painting the seventeenth century witnessed the broadening of artistic interests. From churches and palaces architects began, in response to the growing importance of people other than ecclesiastics and princes, to devote their attention to *public,* that is, popular needs. City squares, group con-

struction, domestic houses came to be thought worthy
of artistic expression. With genre painting, the Dutch
masters brought art down from exalted heights to the
people. New dignity and a new sense of worth came
to humbler aspects of life. So, too, a new impulse came
to give beauty and taste to the utensils of civilized life—
to furniture and the other equipment of the household.
At first, as with architecture and painting, this movement came from kings and the aristocracy; but the
demand, once created, spread, as in other realms down-
ward, until in our own time, it is reaching the humblest
people.

In 1661, Louis XIV founded the Gobelins manu-
factory, where carpets, tapestries, and other stuffs were
made; this industry also produced furniture, candela-
bra, and metal work of a decorative character. "The
transformation of furniture shows how intelligently
craftsmen appreciated the taste of the day and the requirements of comfort; chairs, tables, and bureaux
take forms in which grace and utility are happily
combined; the backs and arms of chairs are inflected
to support the human body, the ingenious seats con-
trived at this period seem to have retained the very
attitudes of conversationalists." Cabinet makers, like
Boulle, made pieces encrusted with copper and brass,
and inlaid with tortoise-shell and semi-precious stones.
Bronze and marble workers, metal chasers, gold and
silversmiths, glass and mirror producers combined to
give the furniture and the decorative arts of France a
world reputation, and attached the name of "Louis
Quatorze" to the mode.

During this century, the invention of knitting occurred, an important industrial change which contributed effectively to an innovation in the convention of clothes. The knitting of stockings led, gradually, to the replacement of doublet and hose, for men's apparel, by breeches and stockings. French production of silk and lace, so ardently fostered by Colbert, also contributed appreciably to the new customs in clothes. The growing habit of smoking stimulated the potters to the manufacture of clay pipes. New and more varied uses for dishes led to a great development in the production of pottery and porcelain. Annual exhibitions of all these products at the Royal Academy, indicated that works of artistic merit were appealing to a much wider circle than formerly; they were no longer destined for the satisfaction of a few great patrons, but for the interest and use of an ever-widening group.

Music

The Age of Louis XIV was notable for the developments which occurred in music, although the principal innovations were made elsewhere than in France. In general, the period was marked by the rapid evolution of dramatic music, particularly the opera, and its spread from Italy to France, Germany, and England; instrumental music advanced vigorously, also from Italy to Germany, where an independent genius in sacred music, especially for the organ, manifested itself; and to France, where there was a special aptitude for concerted instrumental writing. The manufacture of instruments like the violin, the organ, and other keyboard instruments was perfected or decidedly improved. It is also to be observed, as we noted in connection with the other arts, that the seventeenth century gave rise to a tendency to transfer certain forms of music from private, especially royal and aristocratic, to public patronage. This occasioned consequent changes in the standards of musical ambition, and in the social influence of music.

Frascobaldi (1583-1644), organist at St. Peter's in Rome, helped to make instrumental music free from the influence of vocal music by developing a distinct instrumental style. It came to be perceived that mechanical instruments might be used by themselves, and in ways essentially unvocal. Keyboard instruments, especially the organ, and those sounded by a bow, the entire viol family, began to undergo a remarkable development. In Germany, particularly, there appeared a genius for the organ style, emphasizing the fugue, with its systematic unfolding of a subject and its "answer." In northern Italy occurred the evolution of the violin. Greatest of the violin makers was Antonio Stradivari (died 1737) whose achievements both as to refinement and brilliancy of tone, and as to grace and form, mark the acme of the art. Contemporaries, and also masters of violin making were the Amati and the Guarneri family, whose best work equalled that of Stradivari.

Opera came into existence in the seventeenth century, and was important for more than its place as a form of art. It was distinctly secular, and to succeed, it must appeal to a popular audience. It rapidly came to replace church music as the principal object of professional ambition, and hence altered the whole social bearing of musical art. Unsupported by the sentiment of organized religion, it assumed a form essentially public and democratic. Montaverdi (died 1643) at Venice, made the opera the most popular form of composition, and with his series of dramas in music, started an interest which spread everywhere. The first opera house was built at Venice in 1637. A vital contribution to the success of the opera was the Florentine use of stringed instruments which developed into the orchestra, and thus played the indispensable rôle of accompaniment.

Scarlatti (1685-1757) at Naples, really inaugurated the use of the orchestral accompaniment and began the celebrity of the Neapolitan opera. In opera, the art of solo-singing received an altogether new impetus. It stimulated fine vocalization, versatility, and magnetic self-expression in the delivery of elaborate arias. Another aspect of the opera, the ballet was developed in France by an Italian, Lulli, under the patronage of Louis XIV. Equipped with royal favor and a specially arranged opera house, he employed his talent for dramatics, and his keen sense of the values of musical means, in a free use of the dance; and with striking instrumental effects, achieved great successes with his audiences.

SCIENCE

Modern science may be said to begin in the seventeenth century. By science we here mean the accumulated and systematized knowledge relating to the physical world and its phenomena. Such accumulation and systematization were made possible by the development of a method of thinking which is called the scientific method. This method consists of the observation of phenomena, the logical analysis of these observations, and a systematic classification of the results.

Scientific method was not suddenly attained; like almost all human achievements, it was the product of slow change, coming from contributions from many minds, and at different times. With the beginning of the Renaissance, about 1400, came a fresh, general stimulus to inquiry and investigation, an eager curiosity to know, and an increasing freedom from the restraints of authority, either spiritual or ecclesiastical. The spirit of humanism sought to revive not only a knowledge of the "classical" thoughts of antiquity, but also an understanding of the classical attitude toward life in all its phases. The classical conception regarded life as a natural thing, rather than as a spiritual preparation for eternity; in its view, the world was good, and human life in it should be a joyful appreciation of its realities.

Humanism, therefore, helped to increase the growing indifference of man to his spiritual nature and his spiritual destiny, and led him toward greater interest in his physical being, and his natural, physical environment. In the casting aside of obedience to authority, enforced hitherto, by spiritual terrors, and in turning to the physical side of existence, human, natural man took an important step toward the development of the scientific method.   Thus, he prepared the way for the approach to modern science.   Various sources for the formation of this method may, of course, be traced as far into antiquity as the time of the Greek philosophers (even beyond Aristotle, ca. 350 B.C.).   Occasional contributions were made during the medieval period, but it remained for the sixteenth and seventeenth centuries really to establish the scientific method.

Francis Bacon (1551-1628) emphasized the importance of direct observation of natural phenomena and the necessity of experiment. Descartes, having brought together geometry and algebra into analytical geometry, published in 1637 his *Discourse upon Method,* in which he applied the laws of mathematics to the study of nature, i.e., he saw the importance of precise and accurate measurement, and the possibility of giving a numerical value to natural phenomena.   In other words, he created a method of thinking scientifically.   By assuming that mathematics, which treats of measurement and the orderly relations of quantities and magnitudes, could alone furnish a rational understanding of the laws according to which natural phenomena operate, he created "a more powerful instrument of knowledge than any other that has been bequeathed to us by human agency, as being the source of all others."

Galileo (1564-1642) may be said to have combined, in practical demonstrations, the observation and experiment of Bacon, with the mathematical method defined by Descartes.   Galileo has been popularly known as an astronomer and the creator of a telescope; it is true that he popularized the revolution in astronomical knowl-

edge brought about by Copernicus (1473-1543), and
that he was no mean astronomer, himself, but it is also
true that he founded his mathematical faith on a firm
experimental basis. He inaugurated the science of dy-
namic mechanics, and contributed significantly to the
growing conception of a universal law in Nature.
"Nature," he said, "is inexorable and immutable, and
never passes the bounds of the laws assigned her . . ."

Improvements in the operations of mathematical
science had been greatly facilitated by several useful
gifts of the early part of the century. Napier published,
in 1614, his system of logarithms, dealing with the
powers of numbers. Briggs, in 1617, introduced the
decimal notation for fractions, which brought arith-
metic into its modern form. In algebra, also, modern
usage had begun with the work of Vieta, a Frenchman,
about 1591, in the employment of letters for known
and unknown positive quantities. Theories of equa-
tions appeared at the same time. In 1624, Günther
invented the slide rule for rapid and accurate calcula-
tions. A Dutchman, Girard, in 1629, employed brack-
ets and negative signs in his notations. The equipment for scientific method was, thus, rapidly coming
into existence.

Climax arrived in the evolution of the scientific
method with two of the greatest names in the Age of
Louis XIV—Isaac Newton (1642-1727) and John
Locke (1632-1704). "The significance of these two
men, in spite of their own outstanding achievements,
lies not so much in what they themselves did, as in what
they stood for to that age, and in the very fact that they

became to an increasing multitude the symbols for certain great ideas. Under such banners was actually effected an outstanding revolution in beliefs and habits of thought . . . they were the systematizers of the ideas already traced in their formative stage . . ." They attempted to order the world on the basis of the new "Physico-Mathematicall Experimental Learning." Newton drew up in complete mathematical form the mechanical view of nature, that first great physical synthesis—the laws of gravity, on which succeeding science has rested until the time of Einstein. Locke attempted for a science of human nature and human society, what Newton did for a science of the natural world. "Man and his institutions were included in the order of nature, and the scope of the recognized scientific method, and in all things the newly invented social sciences were assimilated to the physical science."

Newton invented the calculus, building, as did Leibnitz in his independent work on the calculus, on the analytical geometry of Descartes, and perfected the means of measuring movement and continuous growth, thus arriving at the "most potent instrument yet found for bringing the world into subjection to man." His great mathematical system of the world, the heavenly bodies and their movements, struck the imagination of the educated men of his time, and "spread with amazing swiftness, completing what Descartes had begun." The spirit of the new science was exemplified in the foundation of the Royal Society in London, in 1660, "for the promotion of Physico-Mathematicall Experimental Learning."

Closely paralleling some of the work of Newton, was the contribution of the German Leibnitz (1646-1716). A philosopher and mathematician, he also sought a method of thinking. He set out to learn of the "old and new ways of Nature," publishing in 1667, his *Novus Methodus*. He was interested in almost every phase of the new science, and discovered independently of Newton the differential calculus; he also invented a successful machine for computation. Like Descartes and Newton, he came to that conclusion which was fundamental in science—namely, that Nature could be explained only by the mechanical conceptions of magnitude, figure, and motion.

While the scientific method was being defined and so grandly applied, numerous aspects of Nature were yielding to the investigations and experiments of a host of seekers. Harvey, in 1628, had discovered the circulation of the blood, which was the point of departure for the science of medicine; Torricelli, in 1643, investigated the atmosphere and constructed a barometer; Guericke (1602-1686) constructed an air-pump; Roemer, between 1676 and 1695, investigated the velocity of light. Gilbert had begun, in 1600, the scientific approach to the study of electricity in his treatise on magnetism. The efforts of many other men were unearthing a knowledge of the composition and transformation of substances, which led to the supercession of alchemy by chemistry. Tachenius, a German, had defined the term "salt" and introduced qualitative analysis; Van Helmont (1577-1644) had used the term "gas" and proved that metals continued to exist in their compounds and salts. Boyle (1627-1691) determined that gas varies with respect to its mass inversely as the pressure on it (Boyle's law). He held the idea that all matter was made up of minute "corpuscles" capable of arranging and rearranging themselves in groups. Chemical change is the rearrangements of these groups. De la Boé (1614-1672) was the first to distinguish between acids and alkalis. Glauber (1604-1665) discovered nitric acid and hydrochloric acid, and the salt which is still called by his name. Boerhaave of Leyden (1668-1738) founded organic chemistry by subjecting organic matter, i.e., the compounds produced in plants and animals, and many other carbon compounds of artificial origin, to systematic examination.

So much information was thus being acquired and systematized that a differentiation into various fields of knowledge, or into "subjects," began to appear. Terms which we now know as zoölogy (botany and biology), the various subdivisions of what was once "medicine," such as physiology, anatomy, histology (the structure of tissues), and morphology (the form and structure of animals and plants), and geology began to appear. It is impossible, here, even to mention all the seventeenth-century contributions made to these many fields, by the scientific method of investigation. Only a few can be indicated. Malphigi (1628-1694), a really great name in the history of science, discovered the capillaries joining the arteries to the veins, investigated the tissues of the body, and concluded that the liver was a huge secreting gland. He studied the skin, tongue, brain, bones, and glands. In his account of the anatomy of the silk-worm, he was the pioneer of comparative anatomy and histology. In his study of the evolution of the chick in the egg, he laid the foundation of embryology. Boyle and Mayow (1643-1679) studied the action of the air in the process of breathing, and demonstrated its function of combustion in producing heat. Hooke (1667) further illuminated the function of the lungs in bringing the air into contact with the venous blood. Lower (1669) showed the difference between the venous and arterial blood. Swammerdam (1658) and Leeuwenhoek (1668) discovered the red corpuscles in the blood, and the latter also discovered the spermatozoa. Stensen (1664) studied the muscles and muscular contraction, as well as the fibres of the brain, suggesting this organ as the seat of sensations and movement.

Collections of "specimens," plant, fossil, and geological had been begun in the sixteenth century and were actively continued in the seventeenth. The establishment of botanical gardens for the study of plants was extended. In such collections, the problem of classification of specimens was important, and was, in fact, the necessary preliminary of any scientific study. John Ray (1627-1705) began systematic classification for botany, and John Woodward (1665-1728) for fossils and minerals. Among the means for disseminating information about these collections and about the scientific studies which were everywhere in process, came the forerunners of the modern scientific journals. In 1665, at Paris, began the publication of the *Journal des Sçavans* (of men of learning). At Leipzig, in 1672, began the *Acta Eruditorum*. In Holland, several learned publications were undertaken; *Nouvelles de la République des Lettres*, 1684-1718; *Bibliothèque Universelle et historique*, 1686-1693; *Histoire des Ouvrages des Sçavans*, 1687-1709. Academies of Science, beside those of Paris and London, were established, one in Rome, several in Germany, and even one in Russia.

To no slight degree, many of the discoveries which have been indicated were made possible by the perfection of the microscope. This, in its turn, had been affected strongly by the new astronomical knowledge, which had caused the construction and improvement of the telescope. Galileo did much to produce the telescope, adapting lenses which were made by Dutch glass workers at Middleburg. Leeuwenhoek (1632-1723) first succeeded in grinding and polishing lenses of such short focus as to produce a really superior microscope. He himself, as has been noted, made some remarkable discoveries with this instrument. Huygens (1629-1695), also a Dutchman, interested in astronomy and in the perfection of the telescope, contributed to the improvement of lenses. Huygens, moreover, was a worker of distinction in other fields. His observations with the telescope needed a more exact recording of time than was possible with existing clocks. He studied the movements of the pendulum, and constructed the first pendulum clock; he also constructed the first spiral clock-spring, making possible the development of the watch. Studying the phenomena of light, he formulated the vibratory, or wave, theory of the nature of light, and thus helped to found the science of optics.

From the diverse sources contributing to these seven-teenth-century scientific developments, it may be clearly seen that the people of no one state or nation could claim exclusive merit in these far-reaching discoveries. It is apparent that science is, and has been, international in its growth. English, Germans, Italians, Dutch, as well as French, and all the others too, have helped. The scientific method, and the mechanical interpretation of Nature were tremendous contributions for a single period to have made; they led to revision of theories and beliefs about life and the universe; they provided a basis for that multitude of specific discoveries of a concrete and tangible nature, which began, in less than a century, to transform many of the conditions in which man lived. While the ingenious construction by Denis Papin (1647-1714) of a steamboat, had no immediate results, by the end of our period, came the construction by Savary, and the improvement by Newcomen, of a steam pump, destined to be not only practicable, but also used, and thus to be the forerunner and symbol of mechanical power.

If the Age of Louis XIV is commonly remembered as a period of the monarchy by Divine Right, of dynastic conflicts, and international wars, it must be recalled that far more significantly, it was an age when the spirit of investigation and experiment introduced a complete revolution in man's conception of Nature, and ushered in the Age of Science. It must be emphasized that during this age, views of astronomy were recast, the principles of dynamics laid down, the science of physics initiated, new branches of mathematics discovered, the theory of mechanics elaborated, much of the theory of fluids established, new theories of light worked out, something done toward creating the theory of acoustics, and the fundamental problems of vibratory motions stated.

To estimate the ultimate effect of these theories, we must go forward through the eighteenth and nineteenth centuries and into the twentieth, where we see how actual conditions of human life have been altered through the translation of these theories into mechanical expression, and how this result has been applied to agriculture, industry, transportation, and almost every phase of human action. The consequence of such application has been that there have been changes in ideas of religion, of government, and of the whole structure of society. Truly, the Great Age was prolific in many things which have caused the nature of European civilization to be different because this Age was what it was.

BIBLIOGRAPHY

Iᴛ is obvious that a bibliography for so ambitious a title as "The Age of Louis XIV" must, in this brief study, be strictly limited to a few suggestions. No attempt is made to indicate the voluminous sources, or even a tithe of the "secondary" literature. Helpful sketches, with excellent bibliographical lists will be found not only in the larger works upon this period, but also in such an admirable textbook as that of C. J. H. Hayes, *Political and Social History of Modern Europe* (Vol. I), and in such recent texts as those by E. R. Turner, *Europe, 1450-1789,* and J. E. Gillespie, *History of Europe, 1500-1815.*

My great appreciation of assistance tendered in the preparation of the manuscript is herewith expressed to my fellow editors, Professors Newhall and Sidney Packard, to my wife, Leonore Packard, and to my colleague, Professor E. D. Salmon.

CHAPTER I

For the general history of Europe during the Age of Louis XIV, the best synthesis is undoubtedly that of the great collaborative work of Lavisse and Rambaud, *Histoire Générale du IV siècle à nos jours,* Vol. 6 (1895). A more recent, but less well integrated treatment is in volume V of the *Cambridge Modern History* (1907). Much interesting and suggestive material, somewhat scattered, will be found in W. C. Abbott's *Expansion of Europe* (1924). D. Ogg's *Europe in the Seventeenth Century* (1925) and A. Tilley's *Modern France* (1922) are also useful.

For France alone, perhaps the best account will be found in E. Lavisse's *Histoire de France.* In this monumental work, the brilliant volume VII, by Lavisse himself (in two parts, 1906), and in volume VIII (part I, a collaboration, 1908), cover the reign of Louis XIV. Leopold von Ranke, celebrated as one of the founders of modern historical investigation, has left us his still valuable *Französische Geschichte, Vornehmlich in Sechszehnten und Siebzehnten Jahrhundert* (5 volumes, 1852-1861). Some of this is translated in his *Civil Wars and Monarchy in France in the Sixteenth and Seventeenth Centuries*. A compact and handy sketch of the period is in V. Duruy's *Short History of France* (two volumes in one, Everyman, ed. of 1917-1918). Announced by Macmillan as in preparation is C. Guignebert's *Short History of the French People*.

A. Guérard's *Life and Death of An Ideal* (1928) is a brilliant and stimulating interpretation of France "in the classical age." J. Boulenger's *The Seventeenth Century* (1920) is a volume in a series tracing the history of France by centuries. J. B. Perkins' *France Under the Regency* (1892) has a readable and well proportioned review of the administration of Louis XIV. A. Hassal's *Louis XIV* (1901) is an ordinary biography of some merit. Newer, but by no means adequate, are the biographies by C. S. Forrester (1928), and Louis Bertrand (English edition, 1928). Bertrand's book is in the best vein of the recent style of biography—psychological, highly emotional, and fervidly patriotic.

One of the most important combinations of source material with good, scholarly interpretation, covering France under Louis XIV, is to be found in A. de Boislisle's great edition of the *Memoirs of the Duc de S. Simon*. Although S. Simon wrote in the eighteenth century, his subject matter deals extensively with the France of Louis XIV. Boislisle's edition is an extraordinary compendium of information and critical analysis. For political theory, mention should be made of J. N. Figgis' *Divine Right of Kings* (ed. of 1922), and of J. W. Allen's excellent *History of Political Thought in the Sixteenth Century* (1928). For Versailles, consult J. F. Farmer's *Versailles and the Court Under Louis XIV* (1906), Cecilia Hill's *Versailles* (1925), and P. de Nolhac's *La Creation de Versailles* (1901).

CHAPTER II

For International Law and diplomacy, among many publications, none of which, from the historical point of view, is adequate, may be mentioned: D. P. Heatley's *Diplomacy and the Study of International Relations* (1919); R. B. Mowat's *History of European Diplomacy, 1815-1924*—Introduction—(1925) and his *History of European Diplomacy, 1451 to 1798* (1928); E. A. Walsh's *History and Nature of International Relations* (1922); D. J. Hill's *History of Diplomacy in the International Development of Europe* (1905), and the manuals of E. Bourgeois.

For military aspects of the period there is little available in English; consult *Warfare* (1925) under the joint authorship of O. L. Spaulding, H. Nickerson, and J. W. Wright; B. H. Liddell Hart's *Great Captains Unveiled* (1927). In French there are: C. F. M. Rousset's *Histoire de Louvois* (4 vols. 1862-8); Jules Roy's *Turenne* (1884); D. Halévy's *Vauban* (1924); G. Girard's *Service Militaire en France à la fin du Règne de Louis XIV* (1921).

A valuable contribution to the study of France in the New World is G. M. Wrong's *The Rise and Fall of New France* (2 vols. 1928).

CHAPTER III

For literature: E. Faguet's *Dix Septième Siècle, Etudes Littéraires* (1898); G. Lanson's *Histoire de la Littérature Française* (14th ed. 1918); L. P. de Julleville's *Histoire de la langue et littérature française* (1898); G. L. Strachey's

Landmarks in French Literature (Home University Library, 1912). See also, E. Bourgeois' *Le Grand Siècle, Louis XIV, les arts, les Idées* (1896), H. Gillot's *La querelle des anciens et des modernes, en France* . . . (1914), M. Hervier's *Les Ecrivains Français Jugés par leurs contemporains, le xvie et le xviie siècle*, n. d., and A. Tilley's *The Decline of the Age of Louis XIV* (1929).

There are many useful handbooks or manuals on art, containing extensive references to larger works. Particularly good are: S. Reinach's *Apollo,* an illustrated manual of Art throughout the ages; L. Hourticq's *L'Art in France* (Ars Una, the General History of Art, 1917); Kimball and Edgell's *History of Architecture;* W. S. Pratt's *History of Music.*

J. B. Bury's *The Idea of Progress* (1921) contains some interesting views on the intellectual aspects of this period. For the relation of science to the general intellectual currents, consult J. H. Randall's *Making of the Modern Mind* (1926). There is no adequate treatment of the history of science in books which are readily available; W. T. Sedgwick and H. W. Tyler have given us a useful manual, *A Short History of Science* (1917). Material will be found in E. H. Williams' *History of Science* (10 vols., 1904-1910). A recent and reasonably clear biography of Sir Isaac Newton is that by S. Brodetsky (1929).

INDEX